HOMICIDE INVESTIGATIVE PRAXIS

HOMICIDE INVESTIGATIVE PRAXIS

Empirical Perspectives and Practical Applications

John B. Edwards Sr.

Georgia Bureau of Investigation (Retired)

ISBN: 979-8-9864873-0-4

Remember, we work for God.
—Vernon J. Geberth

The angels help you when your heart and mind are right.
—The author

FOREWORD

I remember driving up to my last murder scene as a GBI agent. At the time I was a senior special agent in charge who had worked or supervised over five hundred death investigations.[1] At the time, I had written many articles and coauthored one book regarding criminal investigation that had been published both nationally and internationally.[2] This perspective is important because whenever I arrived at the scene of a homicide, I experienced an unsettled feeling that haunted me. This conflict grew from a mixture of self-confidence and self-skepticism rooted in the uncertainty and the ambiguity natural to each case.

I possessed the confidence to transform ideas into action and move the investigation forward. I also kept hearing a whispering voice in my ear that cautioned my every thought and caused me to reflect upon my rationale to ensure I practiced an informed decision-making process.

Dr. Adam Grant describes this mindset as confident humility. He goes on to describe it as "having faith in our capability while appreciating that we may not have the right solution or even be addressing the right problem. That gives us enough doubt to reexamine our old knowledge and enough confidence to pursue new insights."[3]

---

1 Martin, Internal Documentation GBI documentation to support 2014 the governor's public safety award, 2014.

2 Edwards, "Homicide Investigative Strategies," *FBI Law Enforcement Bulletin* 74, no. 1 (2005): 11–13; Edwards, "Major-Incident Quadrahedral: One Method of Managing Investigations," *FBI Law Enforcement Bulletin* 78, no. 8 (2009): 21–23; Edwards, "Inside the Minds: Successful Strategies in Criminal Investigations," in *Recognized Leaders in Law Enforcement on Responding to Community Needs: Utilizing New Technology and Developing Investigative Plans*, 1st Ed John Edwards (Eagan: Aspatore Publishing, 2009).

3 A. Grant, *Think Again: The Power of Knowing What You Don't Know* (New York Penguin, 2021).

This mindset is critical for all criminal investigators to embrace. This notion of confident humility is central to having the discipline to maintain an active and open mind about all things. It is also important for our thought process where we move in progression from divergent thinking (finding out) to convergent thinking (sorting out) the various facts and circumstances of a case.

Reason and informed decision-making are our ally. Our greatest enemy is the reliance on assumptions not grounded in facts or evidence. Our basis of knowledge in conjunction with all other human sources involved in the case must be rooted in the understanding and conformation of the underlying circumstances specific to the particular facts involved. Verification and corroboration become our best tools in transforming an assumption into fact.

Confirmation bias can taint perspectives, judgments, and our investigatory strategies, tactics, and behavior. Existing beliefs can include an investigator's expectation in a given situation or predictions about a particular outcome in a case. This phenomenon is one of many reasons we must always welcome contrary opinion and promote devil's advocacy during the course of our investigations.

An objective mindset in combination with continuous investigative effort, in-depth acumen, critical thinking, and interpersonal skills are essential elements in any homicide investigator's repertoire. The dedicated investigator—their passionate drive, networking, and other tireless efforts—enhances the probabilities of solving cases.

In closing, it was 1983 when I walked into the GBI field office that became my training ground where I learned from some of the best of the best in our agency. Later in my career as the special agent in charge of the GBI Statesboro field office, I benefited from teams of the most dedicated, hardworking, and smartest agents ever assigned to a unit that worked homicide cases. These exemplary men and women made our agency look good, gave closure to many victims, and brought justice to many offenders. They honored me with their service to our state and made me so very proud. In the twilight of my career, I learned so much from these agents whom I was blessed to have under my charge.

In my time as an adjunct professor in the Georgia Law Enforcement Command College, I was fortunate to interact with so many peace officers from all over the state of Georgia. Every rank represented in Georgia's state and local law enforcement was represented, from city officers to investigators for district attorneys. All police domains and disciplines participated in the course with their different perspectives and vast experiences. The networking, war stories, and lessons learned (though anecdotal) provided in-depth context into the operational realities of what we do. So much of what we do depends upon *how we do it*. More often than not, in the realm of murder investigations, *we only get one chance to do it right*.

A homicide investigation is an ongoing process: a progression of timely fact-finding, evidence collection, and sense-making tailored toward finding the truth of what happened and the identification of the person(s) responsible. Often, successful progression results from a proper framework developed from research, study, and the practical applications within the operational realities from past investigations.

My intent is for this book to provide a framework for the homicide investigator and manager to successfully navigate the turbulence in the dynamic environment where these types of investigations occur.

"Noah built the ark before the rain." Preparation is crucial to being competent in directing and conducting these types of investigations. The lifeblood of these investigations is pumped from a devoted, caring, pragmatic, and compassionate heart endeared to God's work and the truth that results.

The book focuses upon four perspectives that are important to working these cases:

- The science of homicide investigations

- The investigator's competencies and role in homicide investigations

- The organization and management of homicide investigations

- Investigative failures (lessons learned) from past cases

Important point: Please notice and use the footnotes citations from the important research. Please visit Google Scholar and plug in the sources to retrieve the full text of these studies. Such will help you blend your experience with the science and promote greater self-acumen.

Forgive me for some redundancies in the text. Just know these repeated terms are intentional because they are that important in the context of the work. An example is the use of the question "How do you know this?" That simple question is the necessary *assumption tester* that keeps an investigation on track with facts over fiction.

Important note: this book is meant to be a reference utility for investigators. Ensure you follow your agency policy and procedure under the supervision and oversight of your managers and legal guidance from your district attorney, states attorney, or prosecutor when working these cases.

THE SCIENCE OF HOMICIDE INVESTIGATION

"Progress happens when theories are tested, supported, and corrected by empirical evidence, especially when a theory proves to be useful."
—Dr. Renee Mitchell of the American Society of Evidence-Based Policing

There have been many studies over the years regarding homicide investigations. Many books have been written on the practical aspects where we have learned from our experiences. What I have attempted to do is blend the anecdotal with the empirical in order to provide an objective and effective perspective from two credible views that come together to inform our profession.

In *Promoting Effective Homicide Investigations*,[1] PERF and COPS research found four important categories that led to homicide case clearances:

---

1 J. M. Cronin, G. R. Murphy, L. L. Spahr, J. I. Toliver, and R. E. Weger, *Promoting Effective Homicide Investigations* (US Department of Justice, 2007).

The Initial Response

- The first officer on the scene immediately notifies the homicide unit, medical examiner (ME), and lab.

- The area is secured, and attempts are made to identify primary witnesses.

- The lead detective arrives within thirty minutes after being notified.

Actions of Detectives

- Ensure the assignment of three or four detectives instead one or two.

- The detectives must take detailed notes.

- The detectives should follow up on *all* information supplied by witnesses.

- At least one detective should be assigned to attend the autopsy.

Other Police Responses

- Computer checks must be done using local criminal justice system network information regarding any suspect or gun found.

- Initial witnesses interviewed at the crime scene provided valuable evidence about case circumstances, motive, identification of a suspect, or location of a suspect.

- Witnesses, friends, acquaintances, or neighbors were interviewed and provided important information.

- ME provided important information.

- The attending doctor and medical staff were interviewed and gave important information to investigators

- Confidential informants provided important information.

Agency Policy Issues

- Make the proper Selection and training of investigative personnel

- Apply sound application of policy regarding the Rotation of investigator/officers

- Ensure the investigators' have overtime availability and their work schedules are congruent to the case

- Provide investigators assigned take-home cars

- Provide intelligence and crime analysis support staff

These four categories have become a repeating theme over the years that illustrate the importance of learning best practices in our craft.

Later, another important study titled "An Exploratory Analysis of Factors Affecting Homicide Investigations: Examining the Dynamics of Murder Clearance Rates"[2] highlighted five key dimensions of homicide investigative practices and policies.

These key factors were as follows:

- Management practices

---

2 T. G. Keel, J. P. Jarvis, and Y. E. Muirhead, "An Exploratory Analysis of Factors Affecting Homicide Investigations: Examining the Dynamics of Murder Clearance Rates," *Homicide Studies* 13, no. 1 (2009): 50–68.

- Investigative procedures

- Analytical methods

- Demographics of the population served

- Political influences

Management Practices

- Successful case clearance is likely affected by the resources detectives have available to investigate such offenses.

- Police response times and the number of detectives responding to the homicide are important police resource variables for understanding murder clearances.

- Although these are both organizational and operational variables, they are also a function of the personnel and other resources a law enforcement agency may have available to respond to reported homicides.

Investigative Procedures:

- The available literature and practice have long been devoted to the practical notion that investigative procedures matter most.

- Although different aspects of investigative strategy have often been examined, perhaps the most paramount areas examined include, but are not limited to, the following:

- The availability of witnesses and effective investigation of the information they provide

- Determination of any relationship between the victim and offender

- Detective experience and volume of cases

- Weapon use

- Circumstances and motives

Analytical Processes

- Although somewhat related to investigative procedure, this area concerns the use of technology and analytical tools and methods for supporting investigative decision-making.

- Crime analytic technologies and methods are typical of this discussion.

- Applications such as DNA collection and analysis, blood spatter analysis, polygraph, and other forensic tools but also the extent to which these are available and used to solve cases on a day-to-day basis.

- Significant effects of relational database usage, computer checks, and the use of forensic tools on case clearance.

Demographics of the Population Served

- Within the homicide clearance literature, chief among these examinations is policing strategies relative to victim demographics.

- This notion that police devalue victims of certain demographics when investigating criminal complaints.

- This is often expressed as victims from lower social strata receiving less law (less clearances) than that of higher social strata (the literature goes both ways).

- Other demographic influences sometimes thought to influence case clearance include the size of the department, the number of officers in the department devoted to homicide investigations, and the region of the country.

Political Influences

- In terms of case clearances, political influences include, but are not limited to, the following:

   - Coordination and collaboration with prosecutors, managing relationships with medical examiners or coroners, relationship dynamics with lab personnel examining forensic evidence

   - Interaction and oversight by city or town councils or mayors and organizational politics within the police agency itself

   - Political dynamics emanating from the media, local political figures, and prosecuting attorneys exercise significant impact on police practice and procedures, investigative decision-making, and even fluctuation in murder clearance rates

A Summary of the Research Findings

- Management of homicide detective units is a delicate balance of oversight and accountability that must provide adequate latitude for detectives to pursue their investigations.

- Development and use of analytical methods are important and can increase homicide clearances.

- Formal training of homicide detectives can substantially increase agency performance as gauged by homicide clearance rates.

- Any investigation must rely on not only the cooperation of others in the criminal justice system but also, and perhaps more importantly, the willingness of the individuals to assist the police in protecting the community.

- The findings in this research show significant effects of community demographics on homicide clearances that underscores this point.

- Police supervisors, commanders, and detectives overwhelmingly point to public cooperation as a key element in successful homicide investigations.

These studies act as a foundation to build an understanding regarding what we do and how we do it in homicide investigations. Moreover, they identify important considerations in the roles and responsibilities involved in case initiation, process, and management.

The study that brought everything together in a very practical manner was conducted by Dr. David Carter (at Michigan State) and his son, Dr. Jeremy Carter (at Purdue). This research provided tremendous insight into homicide investigation practices, procedures, and policies. The study, *Effective Police Homicide Investigations: Evidence from Seven Cities with*

High Clearance Rates,[3] examined the dynamics of homicide investigation in Baltimore County, Maryland, police department; Denver, Colorado, police department; Houston, Texas, police department; Jacksonville, Florida, sheriff's office; Richmond, Virginia, police department; Sacramento County, California, sheriff's department; and the San Diego, California, police department.

The Carters wrote the following that is central to our efforts to improve our practices: Extant research has identified two sets of factors that influence the effectiveness of police to clear homicides.

They identified the first set as physical attributes of the homicide incident, such as the availability of physical evidence resulting from the incident and the method (i.e., a firearm or knife) of committing the homicide. More salient to the current study is that they found a second set of factors that can be attributed to the community in which the homicide incident occurred. Research has demonstrated that successful homicide investigations rely on information from witnesses to the crime as well as information from other witnesses and citizens who reside in the crime area who can inform detectives about victims and potential violators.

However, witnesses may be less likely to cooperate with a police investigation for fear of retaliation or a lack of trust in the police. Police can build trust with citizens, reinforce legitimacy, and reduce fear of crime generally—and retaliation specifically—through an effective community-policing approach. An intelligence and crime analytic capability, coupled with existing analytic methods commonly found within forensics (e.g., DNA testing and blood spatter patterns), has been found to improve homicide clearance rates as well.

The research found that there were strategic issues involved, like adequate staffing, which requires a sufficient number of investigators to rapidly respond to immediate callouts when a homicide is discovered and to adequately conduct the crime scene and follow-up investigations. The lead investigator typically has a number of responsibilities on a case that other investigators do not. These include managing the information flow and the case file, briefing supervisors and commanders on the status of cases,

---

3 D. L. Carter, and J. G. Carter, "Effective Police Homicide Investigations: Evidence from Seven Cities with High Clearance Rates," *Homicide Studies* 20, no. 2 (2016): 150–176.

meetings with the district attorney's office on the investigation, meetings with the medical examiner, and meetings with forensic analysts, as well as a wide array of other case-management responsibilities.

The scheduling of staff was also important. Scheduling of investigators should be based on crime analysis to have investigators readily available at peak times for a faster start to the investigation. Analytic-based scheduling can make the investigation more robust—particularly in those critical initial hours of the response.

Moreover, the Carters found that training and development was very important. Optimum training and preparation for the position of homicide investigator is a minimum of three years as a patrol officer followed by at least two years as a detective with general investigative experience. Upon a candidate's selection as a homicide investigator, the preferred process is to assign the new investigator to a seasoned detective for a field-training process (or mentorship) of three months. In addition, minimal training for the new investigator on death investigation, homicide crime scene investigation, and interviewing and interrogation is recommended.

The study identified the effective foundation was generally recognized that the critical time interval for identifying suspects, witnesses, and evidence is the first forty-eight hours after a homicide is reported. The findings suggest that the key issue was not *what* tasks were performed but *how effectively* they were performed.

Their research focused on identifying the best practices in homicide investigations that resulted in an increase in quality homicide investigations and homicide clearances, and additionally, to identify investigative practices that were consistent across multiple agencies (this adds validity and reliability). Finally, the investigator needs to identify the critical factors in the first forty-eight hours of the investigation that lead to a case clearance.

The first forty-eight hours after the report of a homicide are critical to clearing the homicide for the following reasons:

- Evidence is present and has experienced minimal degradation.

- Witnesses are more easily identified.

- Witness recollections are clearest and less likely to be distorted.

- The suspect is likely to still be within a reasonable proximity.

The Carters' research provided important findings that led to critical conclusions that all homicide investigators and managers need to take into thoughtful consideration.

Their findings were as follows:

At the outset of this research, intuition would suggest that large agencies would have higher clearance rates because they have more resources and experience investigating homicides. While resources and experience are part of the equation in explaining homicide clearance rates, their substantive role is limited.

The Carters then formed an important question: Why are some agencies more successful at clearing homicides than others?

- Based on the collective findings, the successful agencies had laid a solid foundation of community relationships and partnerships with other law enforcement agencies.

- The importance of having solid community relationships was repeatedly emphasized by homicide investigators, particularly through the use of community policing, to develop community-based trust during an investigation.

- Similarly, they relied on contemporary developments in policing—such as the use of crime analysis and intelligence analysis—and developed an organizational ethos of working cooperatively.

The successful agencies were more competent and had better capabilities.

Competence includes staffing, training, and the development of contemporary expertise, such as collecting digital evidence. Similarly, the agencies provided investigators with the resources and equipment needed to perform successful investigations. One of the interesting facets of police culture found in the successful agencies was the reliance on patrol officers to perform a wide range of tasks associated with the investigation. Importantly, in these agencies patrol officers were viewed as partners in the investigation.

The researchers then formed a second important question: Can effective investigative practices prevent homicides? The evidence suggests yes in some cases.

Effective investigations can eliminate repeat offenders and reduce the numbers of retaliation homicides. While not the direct goal of homicide investigators, prevention can be an important artifact of a substantively strong investigation. For the homicide clearance rate to increase, the homicide unit needs to be adequately staffed with competent, qualifications-based investigators who are equipped with the tools to conduct an effective investigation. It is important to have strong support and an open relationship with the community throughout the law enforcement agency and with other law enforcement agencies in the region.

While these are easy principles to state, they are difficult to achieve because they require organizational and individual change for which there will always be some resistance to overcome.

Stated again, the researchers indicated that the role of the homicide investigator has also changed. The investigator is no longer simply "digging for information"; they are increasingly becoming an information manager in the case.

Further, the researchers found that investigators reaching out to a wide range of people in the department, in the community, and in the region, as well as a wide range of databases, in order to link them together to identify and apprehend the suspect were successful.

Bottom line: the study found that agencies examined for their high clearance rates demonstrated exceptional cooperation and collaboration with community members via the victim-witness advocate and crime tips initiatives.

Recent research from 2019 identified five domains of a homicide case:[4]

- Involved subjects

- Incident circumstances

- Case dynamics

- Ecological characteristics

- Investigator factors

Involved Subjects

- Measures in the involved subject domain tap personal difference in victims and offenders and how their manifestation in the violent episode may drive case leads

- Victimology

- Suspectology

---

4 S. R. Hawk and D. A. Dabney, "Shifting the Focus from Variables to Substantive Domains When Modeling Homicide Case Outcomes," *Homicide Studies* 23, no. 2 (2019): 93–25.

Incident Circumstances

- Relational, spatiotemporal, and physical conditions that change how people interact

- Victim/offender relationship

- Motive

Case Dynamics

- The case dynamics domain includes factors that police encounter once they become aware of a murder.

- This line of inquiry has mostly considered the effects that evidence and crime scene location have on investigation outcomes.

- Officer familiarity of an area can lead to better street-level connections that facilitate the generation of case leads.

- The importance of case dynamics may vary by neighborhood and investigator.

Ecological Characteristics

- There are varied structural geographies at the micro place level (e.g., neighborhood).

- Differences in culture, resident demographics, collective efficacy, perceptions of the police, and crime rates shape policing efforts.

- Despite the fact that the domain has been sparsely included in predictive models, variations in social disorganization (e.g., racial heterogeneity, poverty, mobility) and collective efficacy have been shown to significantly change homicide case outcomes.

Investigator Factors

- The necessary skills, resources, and work routines of lead detectives that potentially affect case outcomes. The individual Investigator-specific variations in workload, effort, experience, and techniques that is likely to affect a detective's abilities to effectively complete tasks and thus change the odds of homicide case clearance.

- Homicide Clearance was also due primarily to the work of patrol officers during the preliminary investigation, information provided by the public, and routine clerical processing.

- The preliminary investigation is also a critical factor in clearance, as this is the most important time for officers to locate and secure witnesses and collect key material evidence.

Focus on the investigator is very important when one is evaluating homicide case clearances. Two additional studies focus on the investigator level as well as the organizational support. When examining what factors influence whether homicide cases are solved,[5] researchers identified these important qualities of homicide investigators (detectives and patrol officers):

- The quality of homicide detectives can play a central role in whether homicides are investigated effectively.

---

5   F. Brookman, E. R. Maguire, and M. Maguire, "What Factors Influence Whether Homicide Cases Are Solved? Insights from Qualitative Research with Detectives in Great Britain and the United States," *Homicide Studies* 23, no. 2 (2019): 145–174.

- These qualities included a robust work ethic alongside relevant experience, knowledge, and skills.

- It was further emphasized that the quality of the work of patrol or uniformed officers—who often are the first to attend the scene of a homicide—is also potentially important to the outcome of an investigation.

- The quality of homicide detectives can play a central role in whether homicides are investigated effectively.

The researchers noted that appreciating the importance of these organizational factors opens the door to more informed discussion of potential strategies to improve homicide investigation outcomes.

The next study revisited the Carters' research from a high-performing agency perspective and the agencies' homicide investigative characteristics.[6]

In a granular context, these researchers found the following beneficial characteristics that replicated the earlier Carter research regarding agencies that were found to be effective at working homicide cases:

- Structured and active leadership that conveys specific clearance goals and performance targets

- Investigative units that are held accountable by all levels of management

- Regular information sharing across all units, including patrol

---

6 C. F. Wellford, C. Lum, T. Scott, H. Vovak, and J. A. Scherer, "Clearing Homicides: Role of Organizational, Case, and Investigative Dimensions," *Criminology & Public Policy* 18, no. 3 (2019): 553–600.

- Investigative units that are adequately resourced and operate with a team approach

- Specific training and required experience for all investigators and first-line investigative supervisors

- Detailed investigative policies

- A case-management system for investigations

- Mandatory and regular formal case reviews

- Checklists for various aspects of the investigation

- Training for first responders

- The use of a complete crime scene log system

- Strong support from intelligence, crime analysis, and digital support

- Effective victim witness program

- Strong community interactions generally for specific investigation

Studies find that two of the most important predictors of a murder case success are the cooperation of citizens and any witnesses to the crime, and the speed with which homicide detectives, evidence technicians, and medical examiners are notified and begin their work in collaboration with each other.

Research shows that for every additional officer added to the number of officers responding to a crime scene, the arrest success rates increase by 8 percent. On the other hand, for every additional investigator added to the number of investigators responding to the crime scene, the arrest success rate increases by 24 percent. This suggests that police effectiveness increases through a well-coordinated response to crime scenes.[7]

The notion of cooperation, resources, and collaboration is especially important in gang-related homicides.

Gang homicide exhibits specific characteristics (violent nature, large potential scene and pool of suspects) and investigative challenges that makes it different from other types of homicide. The overall case complexity requires the need for more resources, managing unwilling witnesses, managing media interest, and specific evidence challenges.

Gang-related homicide is a consequential action that shapes intergroup relations, the product of dominance disputes that perpetuate murderous interactions over time. Gangs sustain violent and criminal interactions, such as drug markets, smuggling rings, and terrorist activities, as well as other types of nonviolent interactions more generally, especially competition, conflict, and reciprocal exchange.[8]

Research has found that gang homicides present different circumstances for agency investigation strategies and operational concerns. The difficulty in gang-related homicides is establishing a link between the specific offender and the victim that will assist in clearing the homicide. The level of cooperation provided by witnesses is typically less in gang-related homicides, leaving investigators with few options in identifying a suspect. Commonly, gang-related homicides provide investigators with less to work with, which results in the need for more resources and time to gather the necessary evidence to recommend charges. In gang-related homicides, evidence is neither as readily available nor as easily accessible. There are a variety of reasons for

---

7 Avdija, Avdi S. "Police Response to Homicide Crime Scenes: Testing the Effect of the Number of Police Officers and Investigators Responding to an Active Crime Scene on the Arrest Success Rate." *Varstvoslovje* 21, no. 2 (2019): 101-114. A. S. Avdija, "Police Response to Homicide Crime Scenes: Testing the Effect of the Number of Police Officers and Investigators Responding to an Active Crime Scene on the Arrest Success
Rate," *Varstvoslovje: Journal of Criminal Justice & Security* 21, no. 2 (2019).
8 A. V. Papachristos, "Murder by Structure: Dominance Relations and the Social Structure of Gang Homicide," *American Journal of Sociology* 115, no. 1 (2009): 74–128.

this, but chief among them is that a firearm is more commonly used as a method in gang-related homicides and due to the nature of the relationship between suspect and victim. There is simply less evidence and information available in gang-related homicide cases. This results in the need for additional resources in order for teams to adequately investigate these cases.[9]

I cannot overemphasize the importance of partnerships with local or regional narcotic units when working gang-related homicides or shootings. Gangs and dope go together like peanut butter and jelly. These drug enforcement units possess the information or have the opportunity to engage the clientele and develop leads. Moreover, their past cases and suspects may hold the keys to your case. State and federal agencies need to be included and partnered with as well. They can provide the additional resources required in these cases to enhance the performance of the overall investigation and garner the benefits of federal prosecution, such as an organized crime drug enforcement task force OCDETF or the federal investigative grand jury. Finally, ATF's National Integrated Ballistic Information Network can provide essential leads linking firearm evidence recovered from associated gang shootings even if the crimes occur in separate jurisdictions. These leads are especially promising in gang homicide investigations.

The factors that contribute to successful or unsuccessful homicide investigations are multilayered and a combination of individual, cultural, and organizational factors.

While some homicides are much more challenging to investigate than others, it is equally clear that there remains considerable scope to improve investigative practice and harness best practice and innovation.[10]

The broader empirical literature indicates that a combination of organizational policies, investigative effort, and certain technologies can be

---

9 J. Armstrong, D. Plecas, and I. M. Cohen, "The Value of Resources in Solving Homicides: The Difference between Gang Related and Non-Gang Related Cases." Centre for Public Safety and Criminal Justice Research, University of the Fraser Valley, 2000.

10 F. Brookman, and M. Lloyd-Evans, "A Decade of Homicide Debriefs: What Has Been Learnt," *Journal of Homicide and Major Incident Investigation*, 10 (2015): 14–45.

promising in improving investigative outcomes even in cases deemed less solvable.[11]

Most of the proposals made for improving police investigations can be grouped into four categories:[12]

- Model procedures

- Additional resources (personnel, forensics, information management)

- Improved relationships (internal and external)

- Better training

How we investigate and fact-find is very important as well. Research that focuses on how investigators make sense of things and the weight they give to the theories they develop is critical for understanding.

Such science that focuses on how investigators investigate was found in the work of Renze Salet.[13] His research looked at the process of framing and how police officers reconstruct crime. Salet found that "investigators in any ongoing situation face the question: 'What is it that's going on here?' In other words, individuals ask themselves how they should define the situation. Investigators act according to what the situation means to them. Definitions of a situation are built up in accordance with frames."

Salet used research regarding framing from Erving Goffman[14] to illustrate his points: "Frames are the principles of organization that govern [social] events and our subjective involvement in them. 'Frame' is the term

---

11   Prince, Heather, Cynthia Lum, and Christopher S. Koper. "Effective police investigative practices: an evidence-assessment of the research." *Policing: An International Journal* (2021).

12   J. E. Eck and D. K. Rossmo, "The New Detective: Rethinking Criminal Investigations," *Criminology & Public Policy* 18, no. 3 (2019): 601–622.

13   R. Salet, "Framing in Criminal Investigation: How Police Officers (Re)construct a Crime," *The Police Journal* 90, no. 2 (2017): 128–142.

14   E. Goffman, *Frame Analysis: An Essay on the Organization of Experience* (Harmondsworth: Penguin Books, 1975).

to refer to such basic elements. To interpret or define situations, individuals have frameworks at their disposal."

Investigators are able to pursue a line of activity (a story line) across a range of events that are treated as out of frame, subordinated in this particular way to what has come to be defined as the main action (the definition of the situation). Investigators have the capacity to disattend competing events that are not interpreted as the main definition of the situation, defining them as out-of-frame activity.

According to Salet, Goffman also distinguishes situations that are open to different interpretations. This is what Goffman calls *ambiguity*. For errors in belief about how a situation should be framed, he uses the term *misframing*. Ambiguous situations might, if wrongly explained, result in misframing.

Breaking a frame (hereafter *deframing*) is any situation when something happens, an occurrence that cannot be effectively ignored, to which the frame cannot be applied. This happens when an investigator interprets the situation wrongly and thus acts inappropriately. When this break occurs and a new or different frame has to be applied, Goffman describes this as *reframing*.

There are some vulnerabilities or risks with framing. Preliminary investigations that must be predicated on a small amount of information are especially vulnerable to misframing. This happens with events that occur only once and in apparent isolation from other events. Events that occurred in the distant past are also, and especially, vulnerable to misframing, because it seems that the further back in the past an event took place, the less readily evidence about it can be collected.

Salet states that "Goffman's frame analysis might be useful to understand how members of a criminal investigation team (re)construct crimes, how they search in certain directions, how they deal with contradictory information and maintain belief in their (re)construction. The interaction perspective seems to be useful to study how these processes occur during interactions between members of the criminal investigation team and how members are dealt with who do not share a common belief in the definition of the situation."

Salet and Goffman's work is so important because it illustrates the importance of an active open mind that sustains fertile ground to change direction, improve on a theory, or challenge circumstances by drilling down deeper into the facts. Moreover, this science demonstrates the importance of what I term *investigative ambidexterity.*

The word *ambidextrous* is derived from the Latin roots *ambi-*, meaning "both," and *dexter*, meaning "right" or "favorable." Thus, *ambidextrous* is literally "both right" or "both favorable."[15]

Thus, an ambidextrous investigator can constantly navigate through partial, incomplete, or ambiguous information and case uncertainty. They have both the patience and open mind to see both sides, reconstruct, and objectively work to find the most credible theory resulting from their work. This is so critically important in working homicide cases because I have seen firsthand what science has found: "The process by which a solvable crime becomes uncleared lacks any checks or balances and typically involves the decision of only a single police detective."[16]

Motive in Homicide Cases

When human beings, in every culture, seek to understand "why did she/he do it?" the answer is not a mathematical formula but a story.
—Shadd Maruna

An important dimension of homicides is the relationship between victims and offenders. Understanding variation in this relationship may help to explain the context and dynamics of homicide. The motive in homicide

---

15 "Ambidextrous Definition & Meaning." Merriam-Webster. Merriam-Webster. Accessed July 4, 2022. https://www.merriam-webster.com/dictionary/ambidextrous.

16 Eck and Rossmo, "The New Detective," 601–622.

interacts with the victim-offender relationship in important and unexpected ways.[17]

The above research regarding victim-offender relationship demonstrates important focus for the investigation:

- The interaction at the homicide of victims and suspects

- Previous interactions between victims and suspects

- Understanding the role of all actors present at the homicide

- Evaluating the finer distinctions in the victim-offender relationship

- Evaluating the important within-category (of victims and offenders) differences

- Understanding the importance of disentangling the nature and the effect of the victim-offender relationship

- Placing a priority on the need for ever-increasing specificity in defining this relationship

A homicide case may be described as a situation where "the quintessential convergence of offender, victim, and offense characteristics that define the situational context of homicide."[18]

The motive for a homicide can be conceptualized in different disciplines from the psychological state, prosecutors' argument in law, and the police investigation. Often, motive explains the suspect's reasons for killing the victim involved.

---

17 S. H. Decker, "Exploring Victim-Offender Relationships in Homicide: The Role of Individual and Event Characteristics," *Justice Quarterly* 10, no. 4 (1993): 585–612.
18 T. D. Miethe and W. C. Regoeczi, *Rethinking Homicide: Exploring the Structure and Process Underlying Deadly Situations* (New York: Cambridge University Press, 2004).

A motive can be useful in combination with other evidence to prove that a person committed a crime, especially if the suspected perpetrator denies committing the crime.

Proof of motive is not required in a criminal prosecution. In determining the guilt of a criminal defendant, courts are generally not concerned with why the defendant committed the alleged crime but whether the defendant committed the crime.

Investigators establish motive as part of the theory of the crime. It is used in the assessment of offender identity, and importantly, it provides the context for the homicide, assisting in demonstrating the guilt of an identified perpetrator. Labels adopted for motive by police tend to be utilitarian, often describing the circumstances of the homicide—for example, gang related, domestic dispute, and money. They describe what appears to have happened.[19]

A new conceptualization of motive is based on the situational perspective termed *homicide event motive*, defined as the reason for the occurrence of the homicide. It shifts the focus from the subjective offender's motive to the event itself and forms a holistic understanding of the reasons the homicide may have occurred, incorporating situational aspects and victim interaction. Motive should refer to all the reasons the homicide occurred. Offender motive is a narrow, subjective, and one-dimensional part of the event, belonging solely to an individual with no regard for the other elements that are involved in the situation.

The term *situation* has been widely used within the social sciences to understand behavior and connect people's behavior to the context. The situational perspective, therefore, requires that the consideration of the broader context of the occurrence of the crime and the analysis examines the relationship between behaviors and the surrounding conditions.

Investigation of a homicide case does not always identify a motive in the case. Motiveless homicide does not mean that the police do not know the motive (why and how the victim was killed) in the homicide, but rather that no other motive could accurately and objectively explain the reason for

19 B. L. Parker, and A. C. McKinley, "Homicide Event Motive: A Situational Perspective," *Salus Journal* 6, no. 2 (2018): 78–95.

why the homicide occurred (with a nexus to a particular suspect). This is especially problematic for the police because failing to establish a homicide motive is considered an investigative shortcoming.[20]

Often, motive becomes the "North Star" that leads to the identification of a murder suspect. However, motive may fall short of explaining other important circumstances involved that may lead to additional evidence or explain other behaviors and conduct.

Motive remains one of the single most important factors in distinguishing the types of homicide cases the investigator will work.

Typically, motives and the circumstances surrounding many homicides include domestic violence, financial gain, greed, jealousy, revenge, romantic triangles, rapes, sexual assault, fights, thefts, burglary, robbery, and violence from criminal enterprises (gang affiliation or illegal drug trade).

In serial murders, motive can be difficult to identify. This may result from the suspect selecting a victim based upon availability, vulnerability, and desirability.[21] Availability is explained as the lifestyle of the victim or circumstances in which the victim is involved that allow the offender access to the victim. Vulnerability is defined as the degree to which the victim is susceptible to attack by the offender. Desirability is described as the appeal of the victim to the offender. Desirability involves numerous factors based upon the motivation of the offender and may include factors dealing with the race, gender, ethnic background, or age of the victim or other specific preferences the offender determines.

In Summary

My inclusion of this science into this book may seem to be somewhat redundant. However, when the research is read in its totality, many common themes develop where the research accents the practical application in such

---

20 J. Chopin, E. Beauregard, and K. Real, "Criminal Mobility and Motiveless Homicide: An Investigative Approach," *Journal of Police and Criminal Psychology* 36, no. 4 (2021): 716–728.
21 "Serial Murder: Multi-Disciplinary Perspectives for Investigators," Federal Bureau of Investigation, 2005, https://www.fbi.gov/stats-services/publications/serial-murder.

credible ways. My many years of experience working murder cases corroborates the value of this science to praxis.

There are four sources for evidence-based practices[22]

1. Research evidence—preferably peer-reviewed research / scientific literature

2. Work-based research (trial-and-error testing)

3. Feedback from the organization and customers/clients/stakeholders

4. Practitioner experience and expertise

Dr. David Wilkinson of the *Oxford Review* frames it well: "As can be seen, evidence-based practice is a combination of all four elements. It requires that practitioners know what the latest research says and how good that source of evidence is. Along with their own expertise and experience, this combines to enhance their practice. One does not have natural authority over the other."

---

22 David Wilkinson, *Oxford Review*, www.oxford-review.com.

The Investigator's Qualities and Role in Homicide Investigations

If we know who to be, then what to do falls into place.
—Ann L. Cunliffe

One important key to success is self-confidence.
An important key to self-confidence is preparation.
—Arthur Ashe

Persistence, patience, passion, and inquisitiveness are the hallmark of a good investigator.
—Rod Englert

One of the most important skills an investigator must develop is the ability to form the next question.
—Author

In homicide case investigations, there are the "self-solvers," where there are typically witnesses to the crime who can identify a suspect in combination with the presence of substantial and incriminating physical evidence. Then there are the "whodunit" cases, where investigators have no obvious and self-solving set of clues present at the outset of the investigation.[23]

Solving a homicide case has three interrelated problems: (a) what happened, (b) who did it, and (c) can it be proven beyond reasonable doubt?

The homicide investigative process has two stages: first, identify a suspect or suspects, and second to build the criminal case to support and justify a conviction by a jury under the standard of "beyond a reasonable doubt."

Time is not the investigators' ally in these cases. Paramount to success is seizing the initiative to identify leads and collect evidence, which deteriorates with each passing hour. Time is a nonrenewable resource that must be managed well, early on in the investigation. Often, the narrow windows of time to see and connect important facts and evidence in a case open quickly and then shut forever.

Homicide investigations collect many narratives that are polyphonic and merge many voices, but their construction is highly selective to enable a coherent and compelling story to be told. Some of these voices come from witnesses or suspects, but others come through the narrating of findings from forensic science and technologies.[24]

Mosaicking (a British term) describes the contextual reality of contemporary investigative process well. Mosaicking describes how investigators blend and combine information, fact-finding, and evidence generated through different techniques, methods, and technologies to make sense of "who did what to whom and why?"[25]

23 Fahsing, Ivar A. "The making of an expert detective: Thinking and deciding in criminal investigations." (2016). I. A. Fahsing, *The Making of an Expert Detective: Thinking and Deciding in Criminal Investigations* (2016).

24 F. Brookman, H. Jones, R. Williams, and J. Fraser, "Crafting Credible Homicide Narratives: Forensic Technoscience in Contemporary Criminal Investigations," *Deviant Behavior* 43, no. 3 (2022): 340–366.

25 M. Innes, F. Brookman, and H. Jones, "'Mosaicking': Cross Construction, Sense-Making and Methods of Police Investigation," *Policing: An International Journal* (2021).

The most complicated, complex, and contextual major homicide cases I ever worked or supervised all had subsequent convictions rooted in the "mosaicking" activities of exemplary GBI agents. The Walthourville mass murder, numerous triple and double homicides, and many other high-profile homicides in my career all share the simple, basic, and fundamental process of investigators *or* the sole investigator "putting all the pieces together into one." One of the most important factors during these briefs with multiple investigators is the basic question, "How do we know?" The intent of this question is to satisfy the simple goal of verifying or confirming an assumption with an articulation of the underlying circumstances that support the assumption, interpretation, or theory. This concept is redundant throughout this book because of the immense importance of its utility in cases. I cannot overemphasize the many times we dodged catastrophe and enjoyed great success because Special Agent Tracy Sands, who was one of the best homicide investigators I ever supervised, held everyone accountable by saying, "OK, now, tell me how we know that?" This question during a briefing became a tremendously important dynamic to following verified and solid leads and not running BS leads. Such a process saved valuable time and provided the investigative depth to seize the initiative in that first forty-eight to seventy-two hours from the time of the incident.

In all homicide cases, detectives work toward "sense-making" by evaluating multiple physical, digital, and informational artifacts together to formulate case narratives. The concept of mosaicking is to illustrate how different modes of information, deriving from different investigative methods, are used in concert at key moments of the investigative process—defining what type of crime has occurred, the incrimination and elimination of suspects, and decisions to charge key suspects. Through processes of convergent and divergent mosaicking, detectives are able to lean on difference kinds of facts and evidence to reinforce or connect key theories in the case.[26]

Abduction is the first stage of any investigation, where investigators work to generate theories that are later analyzed and evaluated in the context of

---

26 M. Innes, F. Brookman, and H. Jones, "Mosaicking."

the case. Abduction is "the process of forming explanatory hypotheses."[27] Abductive logic allows for qualified and pragmatic guessing. Abductive reasoning is to presume potential facts by using supporting facts.

There is a four-step logical progression involved. First, identify all alternative evidence, fact patterns, and explanations. Second, examine the different sources, leaving no stone unturned. Third is to deduce and induce the foretelling fact patterns from the diverse number of theories tested. Fourth, move forward to confirm or disprove those theories.

This concept goes back to the previous section, where the science was captured by Salet and Goffman on the process and progression of framing in these cases.

From the start, homicide investigators are fact finders. We are dedicated to finding the objective truth. Such devotion requires competence, credibility, and commitment. Investigators must be objective and open minded, welcome debate, analyze, and constantly seek truth over ego, bias, or opinion. We must be loyal to the truth in all cases. No matter where or to whom it leads us. We must always follow the facts, whether they lead us toward incrimination or the exoneration of a suspect. An ethical and professional homicide investigator places just as much or more emphasis and priority on the exoneration of a suspect as the incrimination of a suspect.

Fact-finding should be a deliberately skeptical inquiry that evolves from general to specific in scope. The object is to excavate the contextual features of one's perspective of a given observation or experience that reflects reality. Questions should be used to drill down into the specificity of the issue and measure the credibility of responses. Central to testing the validity of any proposition, account, or statement is the opportunity to challenge all sources. An evaluation of all facts gathered should be vetted in independent corroboration and other evidence.

Fact-finding is the essential architecture to build investigations. Fact-finding becomes the oxygen, our sense-making is the fuel, and the subsequent theory is the heat to develop the continuous flame for the ongoing process of critical thinking. This perpetual fire should burn red. I like the

---

27 C. S. Peirce, *Pragmatism and Pragmaticism*, vol. 5 (Cambridge: Belknap Press of Harvard University Press, 1965).

RED model of critical thinking. The *R* stands for "recognize assumptions," *E* stands for "evaluate arguments," and *D* stands for "draw conclusions."[28] Such a structured process serves as guardrails to keep the investigation on the right road.

A great perspective that needs to be married into the fact-finding process comes from the words of Judge Charles E. Clark[29]; it embraces a healthy and critically important perspective: "To suggest problems and raise doubts, rather than to resolve confusion; to disturb thought, rather than to dispense legal or moral truth." In other words, the devil's advocate is our ally and provides credibility in all homicide investigations. Devil's advocacy is a central ingredient in confident or intellectual humility and the term I coined earlier as *investigative ambidexterity*. The concept of investigative ambidexterity provides the mindset and qualified patience for the investigator to think through conflicting fact patterns or issues while balancing all circumstances in an objective manner.

These concepts are central to the investigator's ability to sustain confident or intellectual humility.

Four distinct but intercorrelated aspects of intellectual humility:[30]

- Having respect for other viewpoints

- Not being intellectually overconfident

- Being able to separate one's ego from one's intellect

- The willingness to revise one's own viewpoint

---

28 G. Watson and E. M. Glaser, *Watson-Glaser II Critical Thinking Appraisal: Technical Manual and User's Guide* (City of Publication: London Pearson, 2010).

29 Clark, "State Law in the Federal Courts: The Brooding Omnipresence of *Erie v. Tompkins*," *Yale Law Journal* 267, no. 55 (1946): 268–69.

30 E. J. Krumrei-Mancuso and S. V. Rouse, "The Development and Validation of the Comprehensive Intellectual Humility Scale," *Journal of Personality Assessment* 98, no. 2 (2016): 209–221.

This section demonstrates how so much depends upon the competency and confidence of the investigator.

Actor Dennis Franz, who portrays the character of detective Andrew Sipowicz Sr. in the ABC television show *NYPD Blue*, conveyed his writer's script into our professional reality in this statement: "Develop multiple hypotheses—which will inevitably have varying levels of confidence or probability. Hold these multiple coherent theories in your head at the same time. Do not commit to any single possibility too early. Seek truth and facts—which will inevitably support or conflict with previously held assumptions or beliefs. As you process feedback—create new, adapt old, or discard possibilities."

The character's description of what we do in criminal investigations illustrates an accurate progression of our responsibilities. To complement this process, the investigator must have the work ethic, motivation, and dedication to invest the effort to move the case forward in a thorough, complete, and timely manner.

In the mid-eighties I attended one of the best homicide courses in the country at the Southern Police Institute at the University of Louisville.

I will never forget an acronym that was written on the board in the classroom the first day of class. It read, "GOYAKOD"; it was short for "getting off your ass and knocking on doors." Getting out and shagging leads is where the rubber meets the road in homicide investigations.

All of the above requires structure, functions, and processes—and moreover, a mindset particular to one's self-awareness and awareness of others around.

The foundation for structure is the person, policy, and practice. *Person* refers to the investigator's competency and confidence in the craft. *Policy* is the absolute rules or discretionary procedures prescribed. *Practice* is the strategies and tactics called upon in the operational context and realities of our job responsibilities. *Structure* relates to the architecture that the investigation is designed, constructed, developed, and built to constantly adapt to the environment around it. Fact-finding combined with forensics provides the framework for its functions and process to reveal the truth in any incident, event, or issue and exculpate or prove culpability.

The qualities and qualifications of the investigator in charge of the investigation are tremendously important. Factors include the investigators' field knowledge and experience, training and education, and factors linked to their personal aptitudes. The investigator's beliefs and knowledge on operational decision-making are critical factors in homicide investigations.

Character, ability, and commitment are the three central factors blended together to make an effective and credible homicide investigator. Acumen is the investigator's engine to drive thought and behavior. Contextual understanding is the investigator's North Star to plot his or her course through the investigative process.

Homicide investigators increasingly must be able to humbly demonstrate growth by understanding change and admitting what they do not know, embracing teachability, and acknowledging the unique skills and knowledge that come from training, research, and study. A growth mindset refers to one's ideas about the nature of intelligence—a positive and efficacious sense of self and confidence in the ability to engage with and contribute to the world. Recognize that accomplishment is built upon sustained effort and hard work, along with a passion to be better tomorrow than they were today by constantly developing their domain-specific acumen.

Acumen refers to one's keenness and depth of perception, discernment, or discrimination, especially in practical matters—the investigator's ability to make good judgments and quick decisions, typically in a particular domain. Examples include the serial order of interviews, interview skills, search warrant affidavit construction on inferences, or voids in blood spatter interpretation at a crime scene.

In this realm, understanding the value in an objective perspective and perception becomes very important in the investigator's repertoire. Perspective is one's point of view, or the opportunity and ability to see and be aware of your surroundings. It's the way you look at something.

While perception is how you perceive and understand the world, your interpretation forms your perspective. Experience, knowledge, and biases may factor into the overall equation. Implicit attitudes (where bias occurs) are positive and negative evaluations that occur outside of our conscious awareness and control. The number one bias that traps investigators and can lead to absolute disaster is the confirmation bias. This involves the tendency to search for or interpret information in a way that confirms one's preconceptions, ideas, or assumptions, and then actively seeking out and assigning more weight to evidence that confirms your assumption or theory, while ignoring or underweighting the evidence that could disconfirm your assumption or theory. Bottom line: it involves favoring information that confirms previously existing beliefs or biases.

Then there is tunnel vision, which tends to come about as a result of an investigator's lack of the cognitive resources or ability to understand the context and environment and to process facts and circumstances. These investigators tend to have trouble understanding the reality of the situation in all its complexity and create a simpler version of reality based on their beliefs.

Three more regularly occurring biases in our craft are as follows:

- **Availability:** the easier the information is to recall, the more weight you will give it (personal or anecdotal experiences)

- **Anchoring:** the tendency to anchor on an initial estimate and fail to adjust for actual uncertainty

- **Representative:** whether the object or person seems typical of a category (just because something is plausible doesn't mean it's probable)

These biases demonstrate the importance of an investigator's ability to integrate new information into their current set of beliefs and the willingness to change their existing beliefs according to the strength of evidence that supports them.

The investigator must think flexibly and see things from multiple angles in order to deal with the full range of issues they will inevitably encounter. Homicide cases are at once complicated, contextual, and ambiguous. Active open-mindedness helps the investigator see all the angles in situations and issues by looking through different perspectives. The investigator is required to see the possibilities they did not see or think about before. Such requires investigators to maintain the ability to remain self-aware in four areas:

- **Introspection:** a reflective looking inward; an examination of one's own thoughts and feelings

- **Insight:** the power or act of seeing into a situation

- **Perspective:** your point of view, the opportunity and ability to see and be aware of your surroundings, or the way you look at something.

- **Perception:** how you perceive and understand the world; your interpretation from your perspective (experience, knowledge, and biases may factor into the overall equation)

Objectivity helps one see, read situations, identify influences, understand nuances, and weigh different options or alternatives. Reflection synthesizes information and data in a way that drives new insights for an investigator to understand context and work through complexity.

An excellent example comes with the language in a study on confirmation bias in criminal investigations. The study found that the primary challenge for researchers and policy makers should therefore not be the impracticable tasks of making investigators avoid using case-specific hypotheses as investigative tools. Rather, it should be of interest to develop increasingly objective investigative methods and to alleviate the pressures toward confirmatory thinking posed by investigators' work environment.[31]

One of the most effective strategies for reducing judgmental biases is to make investigators systematically consider alternatives.[32]

---

31   K. Ask and P. A. Granhag, "Motivational Sources of Confirmation Bias in Criminal Investigations: The Need for Cognitive Closure," *Journal of Investigative Psychology and Offender Profiling* 2, no. 1 (2005): 43–63.

32   B. Fischhoff, "Hindsight Is Not Equal to Foresight: The Effect of Outcome Knowledge on Judgment under Uncertainty," *Journal of Experimental Psychology: Human Perception and Performance* 1, no. 3 (1975): 288–299.

Contextual knowledge is knowing the bigger picture, knowing the way all the pieces fit together and how they influence change. An investigator with an active open mindset has three skillsets:

- **Absorptive capacity:** the ability to value, assimilate, and apply new knowledge for learning and problem-solving

- **Cognitive control:** helps individuals in overcoming automatic response sets in favor of a more appropriate contextual response

- **Cognitive flexibility:** the ability to cognitively control and shift mental mindsets

As Vernon Geberth would say, "Previous experience is invaluable but can become a hindrance when allowance is not made for new possibilities. Each case is distinct and unique and may require a fresh approach or perspective. Keep an open mind."

I save the most important quality of a competent investigator for last. This is the habit of using the Socratic method of questioning to ensure assumptions are tested and found to be credible.

I have found after over forty-five years of law enforcement experience that the most important question we can ask is, *"How do you know."* This question demands us and others to provide a basis of knowledge to support our beliefs or assumptions. It requires us to articulate the underlying facts and circumstances to support our conclusions. Credible investigations depend on the information being fact based and conclusions being supported by evidence.

Sound investigations depend upon investigators:

- promoting objectivity and open-mindedness,

- drawing conclusions based on articulable facts,

- saying when "we know" and "when we don't know,"

- preaching the value of independent corroboration,

- demanding verification over opinion,

- preaching a general to specific "patient" observation of all things, and

- reminding everyone of the importance of nuance in what we see and hear—or don't...

I also found that our thought process should progress from a divergent-thinking mode where we try "finding out" (where we are nonjudgmental, open to listening, and work to research and weigh all theories). Then, once we have all the facts and circumstances available, we progress into a convergent-thinking mode, where we sort out those facts (we look at the overall totality of all the facts and circumstances for the most reasonable theory that the evidence supports).

The lead investigator must frame this process by taking the following actions:

- Promoting investigative objectivity and case open-mindedness

- Drawing conclusions based on articulable facts, supported by evidence

- Be comfortable to say when "we know" and "when we don't know"

- Preach the value and need for independent corroboration

- Ensure objective verification over subjective opinion

- Preach a general to specific process with a "patient" observation of all things

- Remind everyone the importance of nuance in what we see, hear, are told, or not

The Dangers of Preliminary Information

In the progression of a homicide investigative process, information is acquired sequentially. Often, preliminary information influences the assessment of later information. Fahsing frames it best: "A central problem, therefore, is story-construction based on subsets, rather than the sum, of the evidence. Evidence discovered late in an investigation is therefore less likely to be evaluated in an unbiased way, and conflicting information that fails to support the initial hypotheses, or lines of enquiry, may be discovered but rejected, or not even discovered."[33]

Investigators form hypotheses based upon a thorough evaluation of the available information and evidence available in a case. Then investigators work to make credible inferences drawn from the facts and circumstances they have uncovered. Preliminary information is the starting place for all inquiries. All preliminary information received should go through a vetting or distillation process before it is believed. Unfortunately, it is sometimes taken at face value and evolves with a momentum of its own. We can easily become prisoner to subjective assumptions because they are often rooted in feelings that spring up at the beginning of the incident or information provided to the investigator absent the messenger having the basis of knowledge or an underlying factual knowledge of the reality in the case. These untested assumptions spawn stories, narratives, or rumors that are quickly incorporated into case theories. By their very nature of acceptance and belief, investigators will spend less time and work to verify the specifics that they rely on. Often, these assumptions become the door to failure.

This is why we must take the time and effort to thoroughly complete the difficult work to uncover, analyze, corroborate, interpret, and understand the contextual features of every case and the nuances hidden within.

---

33 I. A. Fahsing, *The Making of an Expert Detective: Thinking and Deciding in Criminal Investigations* (2016).

Preliminary information is often complex and vague. Moreover, many times the information we are told, hear, or receive at the beginning of the case is either misleading, incomplete, or false.

All reasoning starts with the digestion of preliminary information. In criminal fact-finding, reasoning is typically inductive, where you start with specific observations and form general conclusions. In deductive reasoning, you progress from general ideas to specific conclusions. Both processes are important to investigators' methods of drawing conclusions and playing devil's advocate to ensure those conclusions are right.

Preliminary information forms two issues:

- How we vet and discern the information

- How and with whom we communicate the information

We must be skeptical of all preliminary information. It must be evaluated by identifying its source, the credibility or reliability of the source, and the underlying facts or basis of knowledge from the source. In other words, "how get they get the information, or how do they know what they say they know." Further, we must demand specificity in the content of the information for the credibility in the context of the information. Drilling down into the details is paramount to the process of determining the whether the information is worthy of belief.

A huge question becomes how much of and when to communicate unsubstantiated or unconfirmed preliminary information up or down the chain of command or horizontally to other investigators. Command staff needs to have a credible picture of the issue to make informed decisions in a timely manner. Command staff will have external pressures from political leaders and the media to provide statements of fact that they will be held accountable to later for its accuracy.

Down the chain and horizontally, information will work to frame the focus of issues within the investigative effort and shape operational strategies and investigative tactics.

This is why the requirement for preliminary information to be verified is so important. However, it is equally important to be able to mitigate risk or seize opportunity by acting on information that is time sensitive. There is no cookie-cutter solution to this paradoxical dilemma. Such demonstrates the necessity for the essential response from the investigator to determine the basis of knowledge of the preliminary facts and circumstances brought forth in the early stages of any case.

A precaution to remember: it is difficult to near impossible to put the genie back into the bottle once we let it out.

It is also important to understand the propensity of preliminary information to bias our decision-making process (good or bad). This can lead to how we as the chief investigator or manager frame the investigative focus and priorities regarding issues, events, victims, witnesses, or suspects in the investigation.

Often our preferences are *frame bound* rather than *reality bound*. We have previously examined how frames act as a coherent set of ideas or beliefs that form a prism or lens that enables the investigator to see what's going on in the circumstances around their case. Frames define the questions we ask and solutions we consider.[34]

The extreme case focus and drive produced by a homicide investigation can cause investigators to take risks or ignore probable adverse consequences. Sometimes, the investigator is so deeply concerned with case results they fail to see peripheral issues. Investigators and managers will fail when they take too narrow of a view or develop a bias perspective in the investigation. Investigators must think flexibly and see the facts of each case from multiple angles—and then manage the totality of all circumstances they find during their investigative process. Investigators must sustain the investigative discipline to remain both objective and fact driven.

One of the best illustrations of objectivity and critical thinking comes from Facione's work in 1990, where his description is of great utility to every investigator: "The ideal critical thinker is habitually inquisitive, well-informed, trustful of reason, openminded, flexible, fair-minded in evaluation,

---

34 L. G. Bolman and T. E. Deal, *Reframing Organizations: Artistry, Choice, and Leadership* (City of Publication: Hoboken, NJ. John Wiley & Sons, 2017).

honest in facing personal biases, prudent in making judgments, willing to reconsider, clear about issues, orderly in complex matters, diligent in seeking relevant information, reasonable in the selection of criteria, focused in inquiry, and persistent in seeking results which are as precise as the subject and the circumstances of inquiry permit."[35]

The way we investigate and how we investigate become major factors in the success or failure of equivocal death investigations:

- Work them just like you would a homicide; proceed in the same methodical manner.

- Invest the time and effort in the case.

- Lock down witnesses early to preserve valuable timelines.

- Follow the evidence and eliminate the "monkeys" (monkeys are red herrings, rumors, etc.).

- Document the key findings at the scene or on the body in notes and photos.

- Ensure process is followed (coroner inquest, DA review, etc.).

- In justifiable homicide cases, submit file to DA for letter of no intent to prosecute *or* grand jury.

- Be prepared for the dynamics with family / significant others regarding suicide.

---

35 P. A. Facione, "Critical Thinking: A Statement of Expert Consensus for Purposes of Educational Assessment and Instruction," Research findings and recommendations prepared for the Committee on Pre-College Philosophy of the American Philosophical Association.

Missing Person Investigations:

- Work these cases just like you would a homicide; proceed in the same methodical manner.

- Invest the time and effort into the case.

- Use the resources needed to capture witness accounts and document statements early.

- Bifurcate investigative and search operations with close coordination and constant briefings.

- Follow the evidence and eliminate the "boogers" (boogers are monkeys / red herrings).

- Conduct forensic searches and document *what isn't there* as well as *what is there* at *all* probable case-connected locations.

- Locate and collect the missing person's DNA samples.

- Document interviews with all possible witnesses, and lock them into stories.

- Conduct immediate physical and digital tracking and broad canvassing.

- Enter in *all* missing person databases.

Strategic planning regarding the context of any case involves the organization of resources and the operational application in the investigation. These initial steps are all critical as they blend together, change, and adapt to move forward. Any equivocal death or missing person case that turns into a homicide case generates its own ecosystem where one issue has its effect upon another. This illustrates why it is so important to work these cases at the onset the same meticulous way as a homicide. As a result, the chief or lead investigator must constantly manage their case as a dynamic and fluid manifestation of human interactions that open doors down unknown hallways that lead to a room of truth. Central to this fact-finding journey is the course taken by the investigator and the work to be done.

People Make Cases

I was a rookie GBI field agent from a narcotics background at Atlanta headquarters sent to work in Southeast Georgia. I wanted to transfer to the GBI Statesboro, Georgia, field office because it covered my family home of six generations. My grandmother had been elected sheriff of Evans County in 1940, and I was a deputy sheriff there in 1977. When the opportunity to work my home opened, I jumped on it. Later in my career, I may have limited my upward mobility by choosing not to go back to headquarters, but remaining where I grew up was important. My wife and I wanted to raise our boys in rural Georgia. My wife worked for years as one of our circuit's juvenile probation officers. Our family roots run long and deep in Southeast Georgia. It's not just the land—it's the people who mattered. I never imagined that the future would see my youngest son, Mac, be elected sheriff in 2020 and my oldest son, JB, appointed staff attorney for a superior court judge.

My assignment at GBI Statesboro covered both rural and urban areas, Chatham County (Savannah) being the urban area and Tattnall County being one of the ten most rural of all the coastal Georgia counties I worked. Romie Waters was the sheriff in Tattnall for many years (he became a cherished friend). Romie was famous for his wisdom and acumen in law enforcement and in the courts. He told me once, "JB, people make cases...evidence supports them." This advice was some of the best advice I ever received. It is worth its weight in gold to homicide investigators. People do matter: how we see them, hear them, identify them, and treat them becomes so very important. In addition, my mother use to tell me, *"You catch far more flies with honey than with vinegar."* Developing and sustaining good professional relationships with people in our investigations often becomes paramount in our efforts to be successful. Especially when they become *stakeholders.*

Often, our attitude may define and influence our behavior toward others. One of the most consistent findings to emerge from groups research is that individuals are deeply affected by how they are viewed and evaluated by fellow group members. Individuals' assessment of the quality of their relationship with other group members is referred to as respect.[36] Much social science research has shown a direct connection of respect to our attitudes and behaviors that affect the positive outcomes and welfare of the group. Respect represents some aspect of the group's evaluation of the individual, similar to the notion of social reputation—a reflection of the collective opinions other group members holds of the person.[37]

Respect boils down into two core social constructs:

- The need for status

- The need for social inclusion

How individuals are treated by group authorities can shape perceptions of the extent to which they are valued and liked by the group. Authorities who behave in a neutral, trustworthy, and benevolent way are judged to have acted fairly.[38] Fair treatment by the police to a person demonstrates that they are respected and a valued member of the community. Authorities, because of their special position and influence within a group, should be a

---

36 Y. J. Huo, K. R. Binning, and L. E. Molina, "Testing an Integrative Model of Respect: Implications for Social Engagement and Well-Being," *Personality and Social Psychology Bulletin* 36, no. 2 (2010): 200–212.

37 N. Emler and N. Hopkins, "Reputation, Social Identity and the Self," in *Social Identity Theory: Constructive and Critical Advances*, ed. D. Abrams & M. A. Hogg (New York/Berlin: Springer-Verlag, 1990), 113–130.

38 T. R. Tyler and E. A. Lind, "A Relational Model of Authority in Groups," *Advances in Experimental Social Psychology*, 25 (1992): 115–191.

particularly diagnostic source of information about the individual's standing within the group.[39]

How we see people often determines how we judge or label them. This often occurs automatically and outside of our conscience thought. Such demonstrates why we must see all people with value and understand how important our attitude becomes in our interactions, behavior, and decision-making. We must follow the golden rule and treat people like we would want to be treated.

This concept applies to all victims, witnesses, or suspects in all cases. We take an oath to uphold the constitution to protect citizens' rights. Whether it be the search and seizure laws regarding the Fourth Amendment or their first and foremost God-given right to live. We are public servants, and that understanding is critical to develop our attitude toward others who may be different from us.

We must ensure that we demonstrate a continuing culture of just behaviors toward all citizens, victims, witnesses, and suspects. These are some examples of what people consider involving perceptions of a fair decision process:[40]

- **Truthfulness:** Information, when it can be given, must be realistic and accurate and explained in an open and forthright manner.

- **Respect:** People should be treated with dignity, with no recourse to insults or discourteous behavior.

- **Propriety:** Questions or statements should never be "improper" or involve subjective bias or prejudicial elements (ideology, stereotypical judgments, racism, or sexism).

---

39 T. R. Tyler and H. J. Smith, *Justice, Social Identity, and Group Processes* (Mahwah: Lawrence Erlbaum, 1999).

40 G. Leventhal, J. Karuza and W. Fry, "Beyond Fairness: A Theory of Allocation Preferences," in *Justice and Social Interaction*, ed. G. Mikula (City of Publication: Berlin. Springer-Verlag, 1980), page range.

- **Justification:** When a perceived injustice has occurred, giving a social account—such as an explanation of the reason the information must remain confidential or taking the time to explain the investigatory perspective—can reduce or eliminate their emotional feelings.

- **Consistency:** The same allocations must be made across persons, situations, and time.

- **Neutrality:** Decisions must be based on facts, not on vested interests or the personal feelings of the decision maker. Multiple information sources will help to create a comprehensive and objective view of a situation.

- **Accuracy:** The information used to formulate and justify the decision is up to date and correct. Hearsay must be validated.

- **Correctability:** Provisions exist for challenging or reversing ill-advised decisions, such as grievance or appeal procedures.

- **Representativeness**: All those whom the outcome will affect must have their concerns considered by the investigator.

- **Morality and ethicality: Investigators must strive for truth, follow the law and respect the rights of all people.** Investigators must remain impartial and fair; regardless of a person's age, sex, gender, religion, or nationality.

These factors help to promote a sense of legitimacy that signals to a person that the investigator and the law enforcement agency are concerned about fairness and justice.

Finally, in some murder cases, particularly in the context of a high-risk victim or one who had an extensive criminal record, there is a tendency for some to see the case as if they got what they deserved. A while back, Eugene

Howard, a great agent, reminded me of the importance in the meaning of my habit in reminding our agents that any person killed was "somebody's baby."

Equity in victims is a professional standard and mandatory practice. There are cases where the victims were dope dealers, gang bangers, prostitutes, or pimps before their murder. This should never ever have an influence on investigator's attitude or work effort. Everybody is one of God's children and has value. Murder under the law is murder. Further, the killer who murdered the criminal victim may be destined to kill a totally innocent citizen on the streets or devoted police officer during a routine traffic stop if not caught and brought to justice.

Stakeholders play a major role in the accomplishment of the homicide case.

The investigator from start to finish is sensitive to the decisions and the action or inaction taken by the internal and external stakeholders and the various contexts they interact in each case.

Lead investigators must constantly manage stakeholders in these cases:

- Identify all internal and external stakeholders

- Engage and establish open lines of communication

- Sustain regular and ongoing contact

Investigators should always consider who and what the case impacts. Upon identification of stakeholders, those needs associated need to be assessed and considered, as well as the potential effect upon the mission. The perception of stakeholders depends upon the process by which they receive, organize, and interpret information. Trust and relationship are huge (especially the benefits from preexisting good relationships) in law enforcement operations, especially investigation.

Trust is important because it allows individuals and collectives to manage interdependence more easily by reducing the need for contracts and formal agreements. Trust reduces uncertainty and helps us to manage complexity. It also permits highly flexible work arrangements that promote risk-taking and innovation. Interpersonal trust is one party's willingness to be vulnerable to another party based on the belief that the latter party is (1) reliable, (2) open, (3) competent, and (4) compassionate.[41] In police terms, *reliability* is being truthful and dependable. Openness is behavior that demonstrates one's honesty, integrity, and complete transparency. Competence is demonstrated by an investigator being able to perform professionally well and meet or exceed their job responsibilities. Finally, compassion is the genuine interest and authentic care about the needs of another (utilizing an empathetic perspective) and unselfishly working to fulfill those needs. Trust is the gold standard in contemporary law enforcement, and relationships are the currency from that trust. Relationships fuel cooperation and collaboration in investigative work.

Communication is relational, focusing upon the quality of contact that people create together. Humans are "social animals" that make *sense* out of things with others. It is a collaborative process. Collaboration does not mean we always agree. We "colabor" together to make meanings in response to one another. The process between people uses both verbal and nonverbal communication (people talk, look and listen in many ways). We construct meaning together. Culture and beliefs figure prominently into the process.[42]

Relationships provide the architecture to build positive stakeholder management communities. Reasons are very practical. The methods and manners by which stakeholders judge another person, issue, or event are influenced by their access and ability to be receive "behind the scenes" or current information. Investigators must remain both sensitive and conscientious of how others perceive their words and actions in the context provided.

---

41 A. K. Mishra and K. E. Mishra, "POS and Trust in Leaders," in *The Oxford Handbook of Positive Organizational Scholarship*, ed. First Name Last Name (New York: Oxford University Press, 2011), page range.

42 J. Stewart, ed., *Bridges Not Walls: A Book about Interpersonal Communication* (City of Publication New York: McGraw-Hill: 1990).

Different people, depending upon their beliefs, roles, and responsibilities, have different perspectives of the investigators or agency—moreover, how they judge your organization and its mission or job. Stakeholders may not aways see what we expect them to see. The combination of care, empathy, and sensitivity to all stakeholders and the environment and culture they operate is important. This demands investigators to identify all stakeholders up front and ensure ongoing and constant communication where people feel plugged in.

It took me years to understand the importance of active listening. Listening for me was waiting to talk. I did not comprehend how when I actively listened to people, I demonstrated care and responsiveness. I also caught the little nonverbal hints. Listening and observing together is our collection point where stakeholders will show their emotions; tell their beliefs; insert their opinions; and provide motives, hints, and innuendos, all through their verbal and nonverbal expressions—words, tone of voice, gestures, and other body language.

When we aggressively listen and watch others, we hear what isn't said.

Stakeholder management is additional work, often confrontational and aggravating. However, it is mandatory and required work for any investigator to proactively enhance and protect the integrity of their case. In the end, an effective case is built on a foundation of stakeholders who have bought in and been included in the investigator's concerns and efforts.

Stakeholder management is a prophylactic measure to prevent problems and navigate messes. Often, the simple phone availability to a victim's family member or concerned advocate can prevent them from making incorrect assumptions, emotionally react rather than thoughtfully respond, or circumvent the investigator or agency to go to the media or a politician.

When problems evolve into messes, prior relational currency developed from the trust and interpersonal interactions provides the insulation to make withdrawals from the various deposits in the accounts of particular stakeholders.

The First Step Is the Identification of Both Internal and External Stakeholders:

Internal

- Command staff

- Forensics and lab

- Medical examiner

- Coroner

- Prosecutors

- Other investigators on case

- Patrol / other divisions

- Nonsworn support staff

- Assisting or partner agency officers

- State and federal partners

External

- Victims and victims' family members

- Friends (in some cases)

- Neighbors or communities

- Academics

- The public

- Public officials

- Civic groups

- Media

Next is the investigator's interpersonal skill sets and their ability to demonstrate trust and develop professional relationships.

Former president Lyndon Johnson had a saying: "Don't ever tell somebody to go to hell unless you can send them." Johnson knew the importance of never burning his bridges. Romie Waters, the former sheriff of Tattnall County, Georgia, in the 1970s and 1980s, also taught me a valuable lesson about stakeholders. He said, "JB, don't ever start a fight if there ain't one, and remember people make or break cases, not just evidence."

Investigators must demonstrate the following attributes in stakeholder management strategies:

- Learn to share relevant information without releasing sensitive investigative strategies or information

- Establish the ground rules first:

  - "You can ask me anything."

  - "I can't always answer everything."

  - "I will never lie to you!"

- Explain the consequences of divulging and compromising sensitive information.

- Discuss the inherit dangers from talking with earned media or others who may post on social media.

- Be compassionate and professional.

- Establish dialogue.

- Show respect.

- Actively listen.

- Articulate what you can do regarding the case without compromising case facts. Talk in *general terms*, not *specifics*, about case information

- Explain and discuss the differences in the various roles and responsibilities of police, prosecutors, and courts.

- Keep stakeholders plugged in to information they can and should know; explain that some information must be kept confidential.

- Be available by phone (keep your voice mail box open for incoming messages).

- Return phone calls.

Keys to the Cooperation and Collaboration with Stakeholders

Central to working to collaborate with stakeholders is to be able to empathize with their perspectives and then work to:[43]

- articulate purpose and vision;

---

43 R. M. Linden, *Leading across Boundaries: Creating Collaborative Agencies in a Networked World* (City of Publication **San Francisco**: John Wiley & Sons, 2010).

- articulate the "common interest" involved;

- feel driven to achieve the goal, with solid but measured ego;

- listen carefully to understand others' perspectives;

- look for win-win solutions to meet shared interests;

- use pull more than push; and

- think strategically, and connect the project to a larger purpose.

Cyrus Purdiman, another outstanding GBI agent, once told me, "It can't be just a job. You must have passion, be able to communicate and build rapport with people."

Additional Perspectives from the International Association of Chiefs of Police (IACP) regarding Stakeholders as Victims:

Victims require a continuum of timely support and service to heal from the trauma they suffer. These components encompass the needs of victims, their families, and their communities.[44]

- **Safety:** Protection from perpetrators and revictimization; crime prevention through collaborative problem-solving; a restored sense of individual and community safety

- **Access:** Ability to participate in the justice system process and obtain information and services, regardless of individual or family circumstances

---

44   https://www.theiacp.org/sites/default/files/2018-08/WhatDoVictimsWantSummitReport.
pdf

- **Information:** verbal and written information about justice system processes and victim services that is clear, concise, and user friendly

- **Support:** services and assistance to enable participation in justice processes, recovery from trauma, and repair of harm caused by crime

- **Continuity:** consistency in approaches and methods across agencies; continuity of support through all stages of the justice process and trauma recovery

- **Voice:** empowerment to speak out about processing of individual cases; opportunities to influence agency and system-wide policies and practices

Justice is achieved when all stakeholders are satisfied with the process and the outcome is fair to all participants.

Do not make exceptions when working cases involving people of magnitude. Follow your professional, moral, and ethical compass. Work all cases with the same degree of vigor, specificity, and attention. Never assume or presume anything.

Make judgments based upon objective facts and credible evidence, not on reputation, status, or conduct with stakeholders or suspects.

Finally, never let the pressures from the influences of internal or external stakeholders cause you to rush investigative operations or techniques that would jeopardize the thorough and complete processes required to professionally work the case. Manage a credible investigation based upon following the facts where they go and how they go. Make judgments on evidence, not pressures. Never rush an arrest, make a marginal case, or roll the dice by taking a warrant without the evidence needed to reasonably forecast a conviction for the charge. Remember the components of a charge on circumstantial evidence: "A conviction on circumstantial evidence is authorized if the proved facts shall not only be consistent with the hypothesis of guilt but shall exclude every other reasonable hypothesis save that of the guilt of the accused. Whether this burden has been met is a question for the juror."

Communication with Prosecutors

- Don't surprise prosecutors; notify them when a case occurs in their jurisdiction.

- Involving them in the beginning benefits both the investigation and prosecution—they may provide valuable advice and assistance.

- Gain their assistance in search warrant affidavit preparation and other court orders.

- Welcome their devil's advocacy regarding case facts, circumstances, and dynamics.

- Use ownership theory; if they are part of the case up front, they feel some ownership, and thus it evolves from *your* case to *our* case (the benefits of common interest).

Never meet with prosecutors to pull the trigger on a case without being very prepared. Know your case, and have your facts together. Support any conclusions you make with articulable facts and evidence. Identify and highlight problematic issues with the case up front. Remember each other's role and responsibility and how such molds perspectives. Investigators are fact finders; prosecutors must use the facts with the law to prove a case beyond a reasonable doubt. Understand that prosecutors look for truth while jurors look for doubt.

The Media
Homicide cases present three conflicting forces regarding the media:

- the public's right to know

- the professional police responsibility to preserve case integrity, manage sensitive information, and maintain public safety

- the media's need to compete in a time-sensitive market.

Recommendations for the investigator and PIO regarding media management in the context of homicide cases:

- Manage the media—don't let them manage you.

- Do not succumb to the media appeal (investigators must put the success of the case above their own interests).

- Use a public information officer (PIO) if possible.

- PIOs need to vet all news releases through the lead investigator *before* release to media.

Note: *Always vet* and provide the PIO with the information you want disseminated. Further, the PIO should never release any information without first being approved by the chief investigator.

- Provide the media nonspecific/general and generic operational information and footage (throw them a thirty-second sound bite or footage of a nonsensitive operation activity).

- Insulate individuals with knowledge of the case details or witnesses from the media and others (prophylactic advice method for voluntary compliance).

- The agency head can put a gag order in place and sanction any violations to prevent leaks in high-profile cases.

Releases that may be inappropriate or very time sensitive:

- Confirming an active investigation or identifying a suspect

- Cause or manner of death of a victim

- Autopsy results

- Amount of money taken in a theft or robbery homicide

- Results of test or examinations taken or refused

- Type of gun or weapon used

- Type of wounds sustained

- Witness accounts or statements

- Statements, admissions, or confessions

- Status of an investigation and the nexus to certain people

Note: *Never ID someone as a suspect who has not been charged, arrested, or sought for arrest.*

Communications regarding All Stakeholders

A majority of communication occurs through our nonverbal messages. These messages can have effect on our credibility and our ability to effectively communicate. These are behaviors that occur during communication that do not include verbal language. One source of messages in nonverbal communication is the environment or context. Another source of nonverbal messages is one's physical characteristics or appearance. Nonverbal communication also occurs in the dynamic actions of the face, voice, and body.[45]

Nonverbal communication can:

- substitute for verbal communication,

- repeat verbal communication,

- contradict verbal communication,

- complement verbal communication,

- accent verbal communication, or

- regulate verbal communication.[46]

Other important influences on our communication efforts include the following:

- **Our beliefs:** Cultural, political, religious values, norms, or morals. Subjective standards and analysis.

- **Field of experience:** Sets of specific experiences or background that are parties in communication bring to bear on the interaction.

- **Roles and responsibilities:** Rank, position, authority within the context.

- **Communication context:** Environment for the communication interaction.

---

45 D. Matsumoto, H. C. Hwang, and M. G. Frank, "Emotional Language and Political Aggression," *Journal of Language and Social Psychology* 32, no. 4 (2013): 452–468.

46 P. Ekman and W. V. Friesen, "The Repertoire of Nonverbal Behavior: Categories, Origins, Usage, and Coding," *Semiotica* 1, no. 1 (1969): 49–98.

Before your communication, get your ducks in a row. Plan your message, theme, thoughts, and words. Write down the essential elements of information (EEIs) that provide and promote your theme. Use these thoughts from the specific EEIs in combination with your specific knowledge of the case and your expertise (mental models) to plan your script for framing your communication.

Framing in a Communication Context

The skill of framing is based on three key components: language, thought, and forethought.[47] First, language helps investigators provide and project focus and the aspects of situations, define consequences, and classify things in categories for stakeholders to understand.

Second, thought relies on the investigator's acumen and experience to use their stored mental models from experience to articulate and describe the framing process. Central to this process is that investigators who understand their world can explain their world to others. Finally, forethought is about control over spontaneous communication. The investigator must have the discipline to be aware and prepare how they select and arrange the words that they use. The foundation for framing rest on what we say and how we say it in the context of the situation afoot. Essentially, framing is "when people [investigators] bracket their experience and give it meaning in a particular fashion."[48]

In a philosophical and moral context, investigators become the practical authors of reality:[49]

---

47 G. T. Fairhurst, "Reframing the Art of Framing: Problems and Prospects for Leadership," *Leadership* 1, no. 2 (2005): 165–185.

48 B. H. Brummans, J. M., L. L. Putnam, B. Gray, R. Hanke, R. J. Lewicki, and C. Wiethoff, "Making Sense of Intractable Multiparty Conflict: A Study of Framing in Four Environmental Disputes," *Communication Monographs* 75, no. 1 (2008): 25–51.

49 J. Shotter, and A. L. Cunliffe, "Managers as Practical Authors: Everyday Conversations for Action," in *Management and Language*, ed. D. Holman and R. Thorpe (London: SAGE, 2003), 1–37.

- Articulate a clear formulation of what for others might be chaotic and vague, and give them a shared or sharable significance.

- Create a landscape of enabling constraints relevant for a range of next possible actions.

- Set out a network of moral positions or commitments (understood as the rights and duties of players in that landscape).

- Argue persuasively and authoritatively for this landscape among those who must work in it.

- Do the above in joint action with others.

Six rules for framing your communications of issues to stakeholders:[50]

- Remain sensitive to and manage context.

- Define the situation in the most objective and specific terms.

- Apply ethics.

- Interpret and evaluate uncertainty.

- Design a response from the deconstruction of the facts and evidence guided by a critical-thinking process.

- Control spontaneity in both thought and communication.

One of the best descriptive statements found that illustrates framing focuses upon capturing the opportunity to provide a story to make sense of things—making sense of that sensibility to organize it and tell stories about

---

50 G. Fairhurst and R. Sarr, *The Art of Framing* (San Francisco: Jossey-Bass, 1996).

it. Such an endeavor is never complete, but it allows us to see more and to see sense making more clearly.[51]

Henry James in 1894 said it best: "Experience is never limited, and it is never complete; it is an immense sensibility, a kind of huge spider-web of the finest silken threads suspended in the chamber of consciousness, and catching every airborne particle in its tissue."

Remember, stakeholders "will ascribe legitimacy to the investigators as long as they perceive that they will benefit from the investigators' activities."[52]

In homicide investigations, conflict with stakeholders needs to lead to collaboration and finding solutions rather than to a situation where the parties involved become polarized against each other. Central to this notion is that the investigator(s) take a more flexible approach to interact in a positive and constructive manner where they produce the effort to improve their individual capabilities through empathy (perspective taking), patience, understanding, and good people skills.

Stakeholder management is a systematic approach to organizing the relationship between the investigator and all participates in both the internal and external processes involved in the homicide investigation, the prosecution, and later the trial of the case. Remember the benefits of preexisting relationships with all stakeholders. The evaporation of influence can be far worse than the emergence of problems.

The professional homicide investigator understands the context that requires them to draw lines in their case. They also recognize the value and continuing utility of inclusion when they work to draw circles.

Case Study in Stakeholder Management

We had a domestic homicide case where the boyfriend ran over the girlfriend with his car immediately after a fight in the house where they both lived.

---

51 I. Colville, A. D. Brown, and A. Pye, (2012). "Simplexity: Sensemaking, Organizing and Storytelling for Our Time," *Human Relations* 65, no. 1 (2012): 5–15.

52 G. Palazzo and A. G. Scherer, "Corporate Legitimacy as Deliberation: A Communicative Framework," *Journal of Business Ethics* 66, no. 1 (2006): 71–88.

Witnesses' statements described a long history of violence where both had been the primary aggressor.

On the night of the incident, the facts from the case painted a picture that showed the female had started the fight. Moreover, statements and the physical evidence from the scene supported a theory that her death may have been accidental.

In the meantime, the case had become a focus in the media and continuing issue of controversy with the local sheriff. The case-resolution results had become volatile within the community among different factions and groups.

The victim's mother was passionate that the boyfriend had murdered her daughter in cold blood and demanded an immediate arrest by the police. It was clear to the chief investigating officer that the facts and circumstances of the case were in conflict, and many circumstances were ambiguous until such time as the lab work was completed.

The victim's mother would telephone or visit our office regularly to inquire about and restate her concerns over our inaction toward an arrest in the case. Every time, the case agent would respond to her in a very kind way and talk to her about the progression of the case and efforts to move the investigation forward. The agent explained the concept of reasonable doubt and other legal standards that had to be met.

The case agent had to muster tremendous patience to manage the mother's emotional reactions and rumors and innuendo from her own investigation of her daughter's death.

The case agent was in close contact with the assistant district attorney assigned the case, who totally agreed with the investigators' findings thus far. Further, the prosecutor found problems with the legal grounds because some of the statements in the case were exculpatory in nature. I was briefed along with my assistant, and we both agreed with the position reached by the case agent and prosecutor.

As a result, the decision was made to postpone any arrest action until the DA could impanel a grand jury for review.

The mother continued to call the office and had become a source of aggravation to all who answered the phone at the time. The case agent continued to respond by taking calls when he could or *always calling the mother back.* Then the case agent would develop his theme at the time in response to the mother's concerns. Then he would frame his conversations, being careful to not divulge sensitive case information and to talk in general terms, selecting his words like he was being recorded while demonstrating his authentic care and genuine concern for the truthful resolution of the case.

The central concept was that the mother was kept in the loop where she felt plugged into the investigative effort. She felt that she was both "seen" by the case agent and "heard" by the case agent, and she felt she could each out at any time and receive a response back from the highest and best source for information, status, or change in the case she cared so much about. The mother often demonstrated frustration and sometimes became irate when calling our office, only to have our case agent use listening and specially crafted words to deescalate her and calm her down once again.

This concept was found to be essential in mitigating the risk of the mother going to the media, activist groups, or up our chain of command to the political realm of the governor. With all the cases we were working, we did not need that distraction and drama as one more thing to have to stop and deal with. This also bought us the necessary time to conclude our investigation and shift the case responsibility to the capable hands of the district attorney, where facts and law come together for a more holistic review and narrowly tailored result. At this point, the mother was told that the case was out of our hands and her proper contact was the DA.

The grand jury "no billed" the case. The mother called the sheriff, the DA, the media, and the activists, complaining and crying foul. We had done our job and completed our case. Our responsibilities and role were complete. Our decision-making in this particular case was over from the case agent up the chain to the governor.

Exemplary stakeholder management took a little time but saved us a bunch of time. Moreover, it provided the insulation to keep external influences from receiving the attention needed for creating false narratives or interfering with the important progression of the case.

ORGANIZATION AND MANAGEMENT OF THE HOMICIDE INVESTIGATION

It is a capital mistake to theorize before one has data. Insensibly one begins to twist facts to suit theories, instead of theories to suit facts.
—Arthur Conan Doyle, *A Scandal in Bohemia*

In the beginning of any major investigation or homicide case, the managers and chief investigator find themselves in the unique position of making order from chaos. Often, much of the preliminary information is inaccurate, complicating the situation. Investigators must act with the best information available and assign resources for efficiency and effectiveness. To bring organization and structure to this unsystematic environment, they must simultaneously coordinate the four particular areas below, known as the major incident quadrahedral,[53] ensuring that these realms produce the best conditions for overall case management.

---

53 Edwards, "The Major-Incident Quadrahedral: 21."

Major Incident Quadrahedral

Fact-Finding	Resource Management

•Leads Management
•Interview
  •Specific focus
  •General canvas
•Forensics
  •Crime Scene
  •Digital Information Technologies
	•Personnel
	•Logistics
	•Communication
	•Equipment

Stakeholder Management	**Media Management**
•Victims •Witnesses •Officials •Citizens	•Structured area •Insulation/Security •Tailored messages •Ongoing communications •Social Media monitoring

The Four Domains

Fact-finding considerations: Leads management • Interview—specific focus • general canvass • Forensics—crime scene • digital information technologies

Resource allocation: Personnel • Logistics • Communication • Equipment

Stakeholder factors: Victims • Witnesses • Officials • Citizens

Media issues: Structured area • Insulation/security • Tailored message • Ongoing communications

Fact-Finding Considerations

The fact-finding portion of the quadrahedral is comprised of leads management, interviews, and forensics. Investigative teams conduct specific-focus interviews based on evidence discovered upon arrival or leads developed shortly after that time. Additionally, they complete general-canvass interviews of individuals in the neighborhood and surrounding areas, as well as of victims' friends, families, and coworkers.

General-canvass interviews create a framework of data to compare and contrast with specific-focus issues. The forensics part of this realm bifurcates into the crime scene and digital information technologies. The crime scene deals with information from all sites if more than one is present. Investigators conduct an inventory to determine what is present (or not). This evolves into documentation of the entire scene and includes any connection with physical evidence present or in other places.

Digital information technologies consist of real-time information regarding cell phones (e.g., locations, tracking data, phone numbers, subscriber, and tower information, and alpha-beta-gamma directionality). Any other technological utilities, like digital media storage devices, are also important to examine.

Investigators need these critical details to compare and contrast with the information derived in the interview function. Finally, managers must ensure an effective leads-management system to process and document information efficiently and effectively.

Resource Allocation

The resource section of the quadrahedral entails the manager / chief investigator's ability to govern personnel, logistics, communication, and equipment. Many times, major incidents demand the assignment of a large number of individuals as soon as possible. The logistics to support these people and the cooperation, communication, and coordination among them remain critical. Further, all those involved must have the equipment needed to conduct their duties. The facts of each case dictate resource management. Therefore, agencies should have proactive measures in place to confirm that the needed resources are available in the shortest period of time. *This is especially important in homicide cases.*_Remember, what is accomplished in the first forty-eight hours is critical in a homicide case. Dedicating the resources, time, and effort is critical.

Stakeholder Factors

Stakeholders (victims, witnesses, officials, and citizens) not only serve as a source of information but also as a group of individuals who either can cause problems or create support for investigators. Stakeholder management builds the environment and mindset for successful case function. Moreover, it helps ensure that sensitive information does not become public and that media representatives receive appropriate, supervised access to incidents without impeding investigations. Law enforcement managers must assign certain personnel to contact, communicate with, and be available for all stakeholders. Doing so helps guarantee that the manager, rather than an outside source, handles any problems first. We examined these factors in detail earlier in this book. Here illustrates the importance of blending these responsibilities into our overall functions.

Media Issues

Media management represents the fourth realm of the major incident quadrahedral. On a daily basis, media representatives have to consider both their deadlines and the intensely competitive market in which they work. During crises, they actively and aggressively pursue information to better inform the public. Therefore, law enforcement managers / chief investigators must have the resources to provide the media with a structured area to feel comfortable and secure.

Conversely, they also must equip investigative teams and stakeholders with insulation and security from the media. It also is the law enforcement manager's, chief investigator's, or PIO's responsibility to ensure that the media receives narrowly tailored messages, guaranteeing that the successful resolution of the case always comes first and information that needs safeguarding is, in fact, kept confidential and does not appear in the public domain.

Further, managers / chief investigators must establish ongoing communications with media representatives and give appropriate and meaningful information to them. This dynamic was dealt with earlier in the book. Here, it must be examined in the context of the simultaneous blend of responsibilities.

An example would be to engage or have the PIO engage the media with an interesting generic police operation or application that is being used in the particular case, just like it was used in any other cases. Key to this concept is that the information is not specific to any suspect or particular fact or circumstance in the case that needs to be kept confidential so as not to endanger sensitive case facts. By providing something interesting but nonspecific, you give them a story without jeopardizing the investigation's integrity.

In Summary

The major incident quadrahedral serves as a sound method for law enforcement managers to employ. Simultaneous management of each of the four areas provides a structured format for organization during what often devolves into chaotic circumstances.

The quadrahedral ensures proper focus and total coverage, creating an environment to achieve the best possible results for the extraordinary responsibilities homicide investigators and their managers inherit.

Collaborative Sense-Making Process

We have reviewed the issues regarding framing and reframing, abduction, and the important process of mosaicking in these cases, all central to our sense-making requirements in every case. Here, we examine how important this process becomes when it crosses borders into the various disciplines within the context of case organization and management. This becomes especially important in informed decision-making before engaging in certain investigative "tipping points" that will have a tremendous influence in the outcome of a homicide investigation.

Investigators are engaged in the construction and communication of knowledge, requiring them to separate the "signals" from the noise to render a narrative account of what has transpired. They do sense-making work as they grapple with frequently "noisy" (containing lots of irrelevant material) and incomplete fact patterns. Different forms of information are blended in a concept of cross construction. Interpretative and sense-making process is central to developing proper investigative strategies.[54] The word *mosaicking* was used earlier to capture this investigative process and how it evolves from general to specific information gathering in the context of fact-finding, results from forensic examinations, and data/digital evidence from various technologies. Sense-making in a homicide case involves evaluating the totality of all the facts and circumstances and then developing certain theories regarding the crime, victim, and suspects. Investigators collect and analyze evidence, determine the credibility of particular witnesses, work toward incriminating and eliminating potential suspects, and collaborate with crime scene specialists, medical examiners, lab personnel, prosecutors, and others.

Collaborative Sense-Making Interprofessional and Cross-Disciplinary Dialogue

Homicide investigation is necessarily a collaborative sense-making activity. Collaborative sense-making is both an indicator of good leadership and can facilitate effective decision-making. These collaborative opportunities provide for effective dialogue between actors, enabling discussion, debate, and disagreement, minimizing siloed thinking. The gravest risk to a homicide investigation is insufficient or inadequate interprofessional dialogue with the medical examiner, forensics lab, and prosecutors.[55]

---

54 Innes, Brookman, and Jones, "Mosaicking."

55 H. Jones, F. Brookman, R. Williams, and J. Fraser, "We Need to Talk about Dialogue: Accomplishing Collaborative Sensemaking in Homicide Investigations," *The Police Journal* 94, no. 4 (2021): 572–589.

The success of homicide investigations often will depend on the investigators' ability to make the correct decisions at the proper time. Investigators may face obstacles to optimal decision-making such as:

- time pressure,

- emotional involvement,

- expediency-promoting occupational norms, or

- the need to resist going from the process of suspect identification to verification at an early stage of the investigation.

The only real pressure the lead investigator must ever feel is the pressure to do the right thing in all investigations

The lead investigator formulates and develops case theory from the sense-making process:

- They use a deconstruction process of facts that leads to the development and implementation of general case strategy

- They filter fact-patterns for the specific selection of operational tactics.

- They Direct overall case operations

- They ensure the identification and assignment of follow-up leads are completed in a timely manner

- They make the important judgments and decisions in the active and on-going case

Investigators tend to be more creative and open minded before having chosen a specific course of action and significantly less so once a choice has been made. Given the necessity of creativity and open-mindedness for successful homicide investigation, it is important to identify tipping points that may trigger such shifts in investigators' mindset and ultimately to develop safeguards against premature shifts.[56]

Investigators strive to confirm their initial hypothesis about the case, sometimes ignoring or downplaying conflicting material within the available evidence. Such biased processing is variably referred to as *tunnel vision* and *confirmation bias*. Tunnel vision, or confirmation bias, leads to tremendous investigative failures and missing valuable information and causes huge "Brady problems."

Two Types of Decisions Were Identified by the Participants as Typical and Potentially Critical Tipping Points:

The first decision is to name, arrest, or charge a suspect (the decision to make an arrest ties you up both mentally and resource-wise; All steps towards suspect identification and apprehension—especially at an early stage.).The second decision is the choice of the main strategies and connected lines of inquiry in the case (the strategies an investigator decided to set out and follow in evidence gathering are crucial; the lines of inquiry an investigator chooses to follow at the outset are extremely important).

Situational influences on investigators' decision-making include the following:

- Availability of information/evidence

- External pressure / community impact

- Internal pressure / organizational issues

---

56 I. Fahsing, and K. Ask, "Decision Making and Decisional Tipping Points in Homicide Investigations: An Interview Study of British and Norwegian Detectives," *Journal of Investigative Psychology and Offender Profiling* 10, vol. 2 (2013): 155–165.

- Time pressure

Architectural Foundations for Sound Investigative Strategies

The agency's proactive planning and preparation in organizational protocols and skills training is critical, ensuring that a framework is in place to four cornerstones in homicide case investigative organization:[57]

- Ensure proactive planning and preparation

- Define and enforce roles and responsibilities

- Manage information effectively and efficiently

- Facilitate constant and ongoing communication

Homicide investigations are a collaborative effort. As such, an effective investigation must promote positive relationships with valued outcomes during the progression of the case. The four basic and fundamental factors described above must be in place early to ensure the course is well defined and guardrails are in place for the investigation's journey forward. Moreover, the above four features work in unison to achieve the following:

- Promote and provide insight and understanding to prevent, mitigate, and reduce the risk of management failures

- Prevent investigative mistakes that may result in adverse consequences during case initiation, case progression, and case disposition

---

57 G. R. Murphy and C. Wexler, "Managing a Multijurisdictional Case: Identifying the Lessons Learned from the Sniper Investigation," Bureau of Justice Assistance and Police Executive Research Forum, 2004, NCJ number 207206.

- Promote decisions informed by sound communication with ongoing collaboration that is constrained by policy, protocol, principles, roles, and responsibilities

- Ensure a fact-based/evidence-supported investigative progression focused upon finding the truth

Investigation Is the Foundational Process

The object of any investigation is to find the truth. This remains the primary objective to all investigators. In homicide investigations, the truth is discovered and proven through a thorough, accurate, and complete investigation. The investigation is the foundational process to identify and interview *witnesses* and discover, document, and interpret facts and physical evidence from the *crime scene*. These functions come together to a common or consistent result that provides the blend of circumstantial and physical *evidence* that works to derive credible theory in the case to later support a conviction in the courtroom. Central to this concept is the standard of proving the case *beyond a reasonable doubt.*

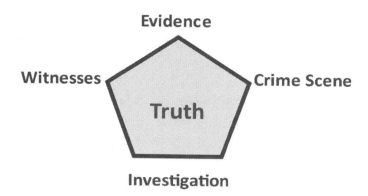

Once our organizational operational frameworks are in place, we then can focus on the relationship with the case and the investigators. The actions of the investigators will define case performance and results. New

York Police Detective Vernon J. Geberth frames this perspective with his simple ADAPT acronym:

- **A:** arrest the perpetrator, if possible

- **D:** detain and identify witnesses and suspects for follow-up investigators

- **A:** assess the crime scene

- **P:** protect the crime scene

- **T:** take notes

The investigator must pay particular attention to and exercise a great degree of care at the crime scene. In forensic science, Locard's principle holds that the perpetrator of a crime will bring something into the crime scene and leave with something from it, and both can be used as forensic evidence.

The Crime Scene

The first priorities of police officers are the duty to render aid, a duty to protect the public, and a responsibility for officer safety. The officer also has a professional obligation to secure and then protect the crime scene for the documentation and collection of evidence with a thorough forensics examination. During this process, officers have the right to sweep the scene, make it safe, and even secure evidence under exigent circumstances, but officers must remember there is no crime scene exception to the Fourth Amendment or "exemption" from the exclusionary rule.

No amount of probable cause gets an officer into a dwelling without exigent circumstances, consent, or a search warrant. The Supreme Court has addressed these issues in the context of crime scenes in the following cases:

- *Mincey v. Arizona*: once the emergency was over and there was no chance of losing evidence, the scene must be secured, and a search warrant obtained.

- *Thompson v. Louisiana*: The court rejected a "two-hour exploratory search" in a murder scene.

- *Flippo v. West Virginia*: the court disallowed the opening of locked briefcase and denied any crime scene exception to the warrant requirement.

- *Carpenter v. United States*: the court ruled that the government needs a warrant to access a person's cell phone data.

Four Major Components When Officers Arrive at the Crime Scene

1. Control the scene. stabilize, secure, and set the perimeters "make order from chaos."

2. Obtain the best and most accurate information possible. Obtain "specific facts."

3. Assemble teams, and delegate responsibilities to address issues. "Clear missions."

4. Provide objective, articulable, and factual briefings to supervisors and other investigators. Stress the verification of basis of knowledge: *How do we know that?*

If required by the exigency of the facts and circumstances to enter the scene, officers may enter the dwelling to conduct a sweep of the area to ensure no other injured victims or suspects are present and physical evidence will be preserved.

Officers need to be trained and conditioned to complete the following:

- Conduct an observation of the area to log a preliminary inventory in their mind (what's there, what isn't there but should be).

- Try to carefully use the same path or course; attempt to walk parallel to walls or places where people normally do not walk (remember safety).

- If appropriate, minimize contamination, consider establishing a defined route into and out of the scene for all personnel.

- Limit, by assignment of specific duties, who may or may not enter the scene.

Central to the success of crime scene investigators is the scene integrity through preservation and protection. Officer must be trained to balance the requirements of clearing/sweeping the scene with careful and deliberate efforts to protect and not contaminate; for example, not touching or walking where there is no exigent requirement necessary, walking along perimeters of rooms, and using same way in and same way out.

Officers need to clear and secure the largest area possible. The scene can be narrowed later. They need to establish an outer and inner perimeter around the crime scene.

- The inner perimeter protects entire scene. The scene is any area with a possible nexus to the crime.

- The outer perimeter provides a buffer for other officers, public safety personnel, equipment, and so forth. The outer perimeter should be as large as practicable.

- A third perimeter may be required for additional insulation from media or for officer safety.

Officers should secure scenes with physical barriers such as crime scene tape and then place officers on station to protect those barriers and to provide security. Investigators or crime scene specialists can arrange for aerial assets or drones to complete photography of the area. It is important to "freeze" the area in time to preserve reference points and the physical environment for utility later to the investigators or the courts.

If the scene has an active or present danger, investigators can request from the FAA a temporary flight restriction over the area immediately above and surrounding the crime scene.

All notes, photos, and sketches must complement each other (up, down, sideways, 360 degrees, general to specific) with a general orientation of entire scene. Video, 3D, or laser measurements and documentation for court from the most recent technologies may also be utilized to complete scene documentation.

The crime scene must be protected from unnecessary entry so that there is no danger of evidence being altered, moved, contaminated, or destroyed. Further, the following list of concerns is important:

- Ensure participates keep accurate notes.

- Establish a log of those who were required to enter scene for investigators.

- Document entry method, path, and course of people who have been into or through the scene.

- Document anything done at the scene.

- Ensure wearing of protective gear (gloves, booties, mask, etc.) of those who enter the scene.

- If needed, set up a private area where command staff can view the scene via photography on a laptop in lieu of going into the scene.

- Have a responding officers' entry list, and document the names of all public safety involved at scene before investigators arrival (e.g., EMTs and firefighters).

  - Record their agency, what they did, full names, shifts, phone numbers, and so forth (for later use by investigators).

- Note and photograph the shoes of first responders for elimination prints.

- The first officers on the scene need the prior training to manage where other first responders to the scene drive or park their vehicles, or step out, and walk upon their arrival. (footprints, tire tracks, and later use of impression evidence or tracking by police dogs)

On the investigator's arrival, an assessment needs to be made regarding weather and environment to ensure a plan is available to ensure scene protection. Be prepared for everything from tent cover to officer twenty-four-hour security if required. Ensure first responders are debriefed and their ingress and egress are noted.

Document those things that will be destroyed or deteriorate by photograph, measurement, and marking. Photographs need to be from general (broad in scope) to specific (narrow in scope), 360-degree "up and down" area coverage.

Make preliminary assessments inside and outside scenes: The physical condition of doors and windows, whether closed or ajar, and locked or unlocked from the inside or from the outside. What electronics or computers are in operational modes? Record whether the television is on or off and what channel is on, whether shades are drawn or open, the position of shutters or blinds, and so on. (Crime scene specialists should photograph everything in general to specific terms inside and out.) Photograph spiderwebs and dust around windows, doors, or portals. Examine what is in the medicine cabinet, what is in the refrigerator, and what trash is found in various garbage bins. Look for any remarkable impressions or stains.

Note any remarkable odors, such as perfume, aftershave lotion, gas, marijuana, cigar or cigarette smoke, gunpowder, chemicals, putrefaction, and so on.

Establish ongoing communication with crime scene investigators for constant information sharing to ensure a seamless *shared consciousness* regarding the details evolving the scene.

Note: There may be a utility for developed geographic information system software for a geomatic location approach for crime scene analysis and reconstruction.

Remember the big twelve at the scene:

1. Watch where you walk and what you touch.

2. Keep a notebook.

3. Conduct a prompt preliminary assessment of the scene (see below).

4. Document any remarkable circumstances.

5. To note what is there or what is missing.

6. To identify and interpret the nexus of evidence at the scene to other case facts known at the time.

7. Plan to secure the scene until after autopsy.

8. Ensure access to the crime scene photography for future case information reference.

9. Depending on night or day or adverse weather, reserve the scene for aviation/drone photography assets (remember the difference in perspectives: a drone flies at four hundred feet and below, versus an aircraft, which flies above four hundred feet. Use the latter for comprehensive overview responsibilities that only higher elevation can capture).

10. Photograph or roughly sketch scenes for evidence, witness, or suspect orientation later.

11. Be sensitive to and aware of CSI identification of DNA and trace, impression, and latent fingerprinting (sound handling, package, and storage by CSI, then to lab as soon as practicable). Don't micromanage...set expectations up front and then cooperate and coordinate.

12. Be knowledgeable about evidence and property through proper marking, proper collection, and secure storage.

The prompt preliminary assessment of the crime scene includes the following:

- **Scene inventory**: what there and what's not...evidence and negative evidence

- **Digital device location:** documentation by CSI, examination, and collection for *immediate* off-site processing for lead generation

Note: work with CSI in their job to ensure their scene documentation processes are not impeded by expediting the investigative custody of digital evidence. There needs to be an understanding of the importance that forensic examiners acquire the data as soon as practicable.

- **Remarkable issues:** important or abnormal issues

- **Scene/suspect connections:** nexus between what is located at the scene with what investigators should search for in the outside investigation

- **Theory of what occurred:** remember Occam's razor: "When more than one explanation for an event is possible, we should choose the simplest…the one with the fewest assumptions"

Critical note: Have an investigator at the autopsy to share information and photographs of scenes and bring back ME commentary to the chief investigator if they cannot be there.

At "Fresh" Crime Scenes

Consider the utility of tracking dogs. Ensure officers encircle or set up a perimeter around a large enough geographical area to limit a suspect's escape routes. (Factor in the time element.) Limit foot traffic, and protect the area where flight occurred. Dogs can not only locate suspects but identify a path or course of travel where valuable evidence was discarded.

Investigators need to inventory all preliminary statements taken by other officers at the scene:

- Identify existing non custody or in-custody statements to uniformed officers, first responders, or other witnesses.

  - Follow up to ensure they are specific, accurate, and documented.

  - Ensure legal.

  - Consider the case-situational appropriate method of documentation (audio/video/written/oral).

- Ensure the statements are collected for investigative purpose and Brady requirements.

Further, investigators need to inventory any statements made by potential suspects to witnesses at the scene:

- Ensure such has been

  - captured,

  - documented, and

  - reviewed and noted.

The chief investigator must ensure they insulate the integrity of sensitive case information:

- By ensuring preservation orders are completed and served to secure text and other cell phone data

- To protect the integrity of investigative team briefings regarding sensitive "active ongoing case" information (limited participants based on need to know)

- Secure or encrypted communications when required

- Covert assembly of other investigators when required

- Ensure all documents and data are secure at all times

- Prophylactic guidance and advice to victims and witnesses regarding sharing their observations and statements outside the realm of the "active" investigation

- The request for the court to temporarily seal affidavits for search warrants and sensitive court orders

- Command staff level zero-tolerance leak policy with adverse consequences

The investigator needs to ensure sound communication linkage with mangers and responding investigators. Communication, cooperation, and coordination are critical. There is also wisdom, not weakness, in asking for opinions and views and receiving counsel from others.

Remember, preliminary information is *almost always* inaccurate. Establish a basis of knowledge in witnesses (ask the question *"How do you know this?"*) Develop the specifics in all information. Remember: *SPECIFICITY in the content for credibility in the context.*

Key to all investigators developing credibility in statements or observations is to *corroborate all information.*

Develop Situational Awareness

1. Observe surroundings in specific detail.

2. Actively listen.

3. Use all senses.

4. Objectively evaluate all facts and circumstances.

5. Prevent tunnel vision or remaining boxed into paradigms. Be open minded; look from the outside in. (use a devil's advocacy mindset).

6. Factor into the overall case equation the history, culture, political issues, and environment.

7. Be sensitive to the contextual richness of each case, and identify the nuances involved.

Define and Describe the Situation

Remember, what investigators don't know may be just as important as what investigators do know.

- What do the facts support?

- What does the scene require?

- List priorities.

- Forecast issues.

- Mandate challenging all investigative assumptions by demanding facts over fiction. Stress verification of preliminary information over taking for granted assumptions. Ensure statements or other information are tested through abasis of knowledge process by examining the underlying circumstances known in the context of the information in concert with the source credibility or reliability.

- Assess all safety issues.

- Ensure the chain of command is briefed.

Develop Specific Knowledge

- The investigator must aggressively listen to everyone to ensure a thorough, accurate, and complete understanding of case facts and the influences from particular situational dynamics

- The investigator's ability to form narrowly tailored and specific questions is a required skill. (*Always ending with the foundational question of: How do you know that?*)

- The investigator must observe and evaluate the crime scene (from general to specific and 360-degree coverage)

- Investigators must understand the paramount importance of memorializing facts and circumstances by documenting in their notebook for later reference, comparison, and contrast

These qualities develop an informed decision-making process taken in context and together with policy, procedure, and investigative process. Training and experience of investigators also factors into the overall situation. The process of defining and describing with specific knowledge development captures the operational realities in the context of the investigation.

The Bottom Line

Often, time is not our ally due to the following two factors:

a. The deterioration of evidence and evaporation of memory

b. Loss of initiative or element of surprise

Investigative management, process, functions, order, and discipline are paramount in homicide cases (remember the critical time window of the first forty-eight hours in the case). Generally, there is a four-step progression to propel the investigation forward as fast as possible. First is to get feet on the ground. Second, size up the initial observations, facts, and circumstances. Third, identify and call for the specific resources and expertise needed. Fourth, develop the investigative framework to organize and implement the active investigation as soon as practicable.

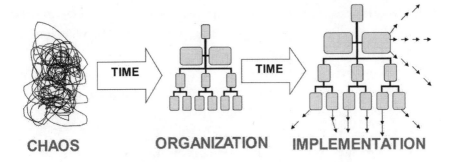

"Make Order from Chaos"

Establish framework and implement strategy and tactics
TIME IS OF THE ESSENCE

The Organization of the Investigation Is Critical to Solving Homicide Cases

The number of investigators assigned will be dictated by the facts and circumstances of each case. A general rule is the smaller the better, due to the sensitive information in combination with the span-of-control issue. However, the facts of each case are different. Multiple lead requirements for time-sensitive issues will require multiple investigative teams.[58]

Investigators often work backward from the event to gain an understanding of the precipitating circumstances and create a timeline of the lethal act. The victim's lifestyle is important in this process, as it gives the investigator a glimpse of potential motives and offenders. The approaches and tactics investigators implement within their investigative teams are very important. The investigation that takes place during the first forty-eight

---

58 Edwards, *Inside the Minds: Successful Strategies in Criminal Investigations; Recognized Leaders in Law Enforcement on Responding to Community Needs, Utilizing New Technology and Developing Investigative Plans* (Eagan: Aspatore Publishing, 2009).

hours is pivotal to successful case outcomes. Agencies that secure witnesses and material evidence and narrow potential motives and offenders within this period have higher case-solving rates.

Management oversight, providing optimal training to investigators, and the availability of resources such as DNA analysis and other forensic tools are also important in solving cases.

While many factors contribute to successful homicide investigations, including some creative practices, there is one overarching factor:

- Agencies that had laid a strong foundation of trust with the community and a strong foundation of cooperation and information sharing with other law enforcement agencies are more successful.

- Without this foundation, success will be limited.

- The police manager or lead investigator/detective must

  - set up an operations location for briefings and a lead investigators' workspace;

  - set the briefing schedule (time and location);

  - set the communication protocol for all investigators to have contact with the lead investigator;

  - establish resource pools (prosecutors; other local, state, and federal agencies; intelligence analyst, lab, ME, coroner, etc.); and

  - schedule annual training regarding the crime lab's capabilities, limitations, services, and policies. Investigators must keep up and better understand evidence analysis and how to work with their crime lab scientist and ME in an ongoing relationship.

The lead investigator/detective should have the responsibility for the homicide case management and should act as the central clearinghouse for all information. Why? Because they are responsible for collecting and evaluating all information. They should act as the maestro of the investigative orchestra. The lead investigator should determine leads and their importance, priority, and suspense time. Additional lead development, parameters, and follow-up should come from the lead investigator. The lead investigator must develop strategy with other investigators and direct, delegate, and move the investigation forward. The lead investigator should direct and moderate the two investigative briefings each day and receive and assign follow-up leads with direction.

The lead investigator/detective must be an integral part and voice in all decisions. They have the responsibility for the primary suspect or custodial interviews. The lead investigator has the ultimate responsibility for all case issues from investigative report documentation, digital recordings and evidence documentation to the case file. They also have the responsibility to ensure all court orders are filed and search warrants returned. Further, they are responsible for the case facts interactions and briefings for the prosecutors.

The lead investigator must sustain investigative discipline in the investigation processes:

- The lead investigator must adhere to the proper operational tactics to further their strategic plan

- Evaluate all search warrants in advance of judicial review

- Involve the prosecutors for advise and feedback regarding legal issues

- Ensure the proper fact-finding roles and responsibilities of others

- Maintain and sustain the organizational processes and investigative progress

- Ensure the investigative team's coordination (and sometimes clearance) with the lead investigator in advance of their follow-up investigative actions

- Ensure the leads-management protocols are in place and all investigators following the processes as required in a timely manner

- Know the realities of the case and communicate an accurate understanding of the totality of the facts and circumstances by all investigators

- Ensure the overall investigation actions do not outrun case leads follow-up responsibilities developed as the investigation progresses forward in time

- Ensure that fact-finding and evidence collection is structured with a priority for subject/suspect interviews with order selection and proper sequencing that is congruent with the overall case progress

- Ensure that all investigative actions do not fail to be documented and oversight applied

- The lead investigator needs to consistently ask the question at all briefings, if it is not readily apparent, *"How do we know this particular fact is accurate?"*

Investigation is a process that fits into a context of determination of fact for decision-making purposes.[59]

- The investigation has an end-oriented goal.

- The end is the determination of fact.

---

59 R. A. Myren and C. H. Garcia, *Investigation for Determination of Fact: A Primer on Proof* (City of Publication: Salt Lake City. Brooks/Cole Publishing Company, 1989).

- A fact is an element of reality.

- The goal must be specified and the investigation defined before it can be planned.

- As the investigation progresses, its work product—the information gathered—must be organized and analyzed

The two processes involved are as follows:

- Findings of fact

- Coming to a determination (drawing conclusions through a process of reasoning, establishing credibility and basis of knowledge)

  - *Standards of proof* (from mere suspicion to beyond a reasonable doubt)

  - *Weight given to evidence* (direct or circumstantial, witness credibility, etc.)

  - *Contradictory evidence, advocacy, and argument*

  - *The substantive impression the case makes on an objective, legal, impartial, and detached mind*

Fact-finding should be a deliberately skeptical inquiry that evolves from general to specific in scope. The object is to excavate the contextual features of one's perspectives of a given observation or experience that reflects reality. Questions should be used to drill down into the specificity of the issue and measure the credibility of responses. *Central to testing the validity of any proposition, account, or statement is the opportunity to challenge all sources.* An evaluation of all facts gathered should be vetted by independent corroboration and other evidence.

Investigators must be constantly reminded to ensure bias, interpretations, or conclusions do not prevent complete and thorough examination of all facts and circumstances. There must be zero tolerance for "shortcutting." All bases must be covered. All areas addressed. All avenues explored. The right people interviewed at the right time. Determine up front whether they can testify under oath that they have personal knowledge. Determine the witness's opportunity to know what they say they know. Answer the question regarding the witness's credibility under the law: *Are they impeachable?* (Character, convicted felon, given a prior inconsistent statement etc.) Is the witness settled or nomadic?

One of the most important skills an investigator or detective must have is the ability to understand the importance and utility of being able to form the next question.

Remember, people make cases. Try to build rapport, convey trust, and develop relational currency. Use kindness rather than authority with people. Explain to them the importance of finding the truth. Provide prophylactic advice on talking to others or to the media on what they have seen or heard. Persons interviewed should always be given the *appropriate* precautionary instructions to keep questions and discussions during their interview confidential. Such insulates the credibility of information and prevents the generation of boogers, monkeys, rumors, false lead running, and retracking.

Articulate to them the consequences of withholding information or making false statements. Form open-ended questions under the rule of specificity, and always establish their basis of knowledge by asking how they know what they say. Did they personally see it or hear it, or were they told by (person's name)? How did they come about the information they provided, and in what context? Answer the who, what, when, where, why, and how (if possible). Assess the credibility and reliability of all sources (motives, character, whether they are corroborated or not, etc.). Finally, probe the before and after issues involved in the timelines of the case.

Often, people will not tell you anything unless you ask. Never let emotions impact your judgment or the demeanor of those from whom you are trying to gain information.

Keep people talking (a five-page documented lie can be just as important as a twenty-one-page admission). Only extremely rarely should you jeopardize the opportunity to go back to a person for additional interviews. As long as they keep talking to you, you learn.

Explain the dynamics of the law, court, and the witness stand. Drive "truth, truth, truth" as *always the best policy*. Remind them they have freedom to talk to whom they want *but...* (the evidence value, investigative value, victim justice issues afoot). Explain in ethical terms the consequences of talking to defense attorneys without a judge present to oversee the examination.

Finally, determine as best you can their competency to testify in court. Will they testify truthfully under oath that they have personal knowledge? Determine their mental state, history, and condition. Determine the objective facts regarding their opportunity to know what they say they saw and what they say they know. Ensure questions complete the process of a thorough examination, leaving no stone unturned.

Investigators Should Follow a Two-Pronged Evaluation Process:

- *First prong*: an actual factual analysis of each fact and circumstance within the fact patterns of the case

- *Second prong*: a contextual analysis of the totality of all the facts and circumstances within the case

When examined in unison and read together, the facts should paint a picture and tell a credible story. Fact patterns should be linked together logically and reasonably with consistent themes.

Multiple fact patterns present common views; the views can be drastically changed by one fact.

Investigators get only one chance. Lack of organization leads to the failure to seize initiative and capture important leads. Time-sensitive evidence can deteriorate or be lost. Examples include the following:

- Cell phone records (locations, digital storage, text, photographs, towers, and calls)

- Social media sites

- Digital media (hard drives, solid state, portable storage devices, and cloud storage)

- CTV video (from security cameras)

- Witness recollections

- Blood on clothing

- Firearms, spent cases, and bullets

- Shoes and clothing

- Neighborhood canvass and witness recollections

- Line ups, show ups, and other witness identifications

- Timeline establishment on suspects and witnesses

- Road checks interviews for "time-window witnesses"

- Crime scenes, environment, and geography

- Preenvironmental documentation through photography

Neighbor canvasses are very important but useless if not performed correctly. Nonspecific, random, non-thorough interviews just cause problems. However, orderly canvasses that are thorough and cover all angles where investigators ask and document very specific responses to very specific questions provide great case value in what they see or what they do not see.

Former GBI SAC Dr. Gary Rothwell says it best: "The neighborhood canvass constitutes one of the most productive investigative tools. Even the most calculated of crimes cannot overcome the free will of humans. When crimes occur, somebody usually saw something, and, often, those witnesses only tell their stories if asked."

Organization: The Formation of Investigative Teams

Teams need to be selected and formed based on the demands and particularities of each case (in multiagency efforts, the teams should be mixed).

- Teams with two investigators each work best.

- Extraordinary circumstances or extra resource demands, such as search warrants, require combining teams or special teams, if reserves are not available

Teams *must be* well organized and well briefed with clear understandings of the mission and the lead investigator's vision for case progression.

- After full and complete briefings, teams can receive leads.

- Teams need the people skills and "*sleuth attitude*" to fact-find, charm, and understand.

- Teams must be well trained and competent in investigative tactics (*or have structured oversight*).

- Teams must be equipped with the information, materials, and equipment necessary to do their job.

- Teams must stay in constant communication with the lead investigator and center for operations.

- There must be enough teams to field the quantity and exigency of leads issued to track multiple theories.

- Teams need someone or a contact with a geographical, demographical, cultural, historical, and political knowledge base and understanding (often, uniformed patrol, detectives, or narcs that work the area).

- Teams must remain in constant communication with the lead investigator for out-going sitreps and incoming follow-up on leads reports or *progression authority* to move to a newly discovered lead or angle.

Note: The investigation must never outrun the case strategy, scope of the case, or prosecution.

Teams must be fielded, assigned, and managed to preserve the congruity of knowledge and work in the case interviews, theory, and fact patterns.

> Example: the same officer's reinterview of the same persons has the benefit of consistent evaluations of demeanor, general observations, and information.

One team member from each team should be a designated "scribe" to be responsible for the completion of investigative summaries documenting acts, events, and interviews.

Beware of the creation of dual reports regarding the same interview or investigative event. Such can cause the development of "boogers and monkeys" or massive discovery issues if retained in a separate file and not disclosed.

Teams must attend briefings with the chief investigator to compare and contrast content and context of statements taken, evidence collected, and other fact patterns and, further, to ensure teams are debriefed regularly during the course of the investigation by the lead investigator for case continuity. Finally, supervisors should manage investigators' work hours, shifts, or work periods to ensure alert, less stressed, and more mindful officers.

The lead investigator must not permit investigators to jump to conclusions in the case. Guidance and constant counsel should remind all to follow the facts and evidence to the credible and reasonable theories based on verified fact patterns. All investigators must coordinate with the lead investigator on each lead for operational continuity, lead documentation, and follow-up.

All investigators must maintain and sustain "investigative discipline" with a qualified patience in their efforts within the context of the overall investigation. Special Agent Chuck Sullenger, another exemplary agent at our office, used to frame it well: "The case agent (chief investigator) should be someone who understands the phrase 'What's important now.'"

It Is Critically Important for Investigative Teams to Locate and Interview *All* Potential Witnesses Quickly

- Lock them into statements.

- Locate and preserve evidence.

- Obtain the most accurate accounts and timelines.

- Preserve reference windows of time.

- Seek independent corroboration of statements.

- Tie down lead and close or follow up on additional leads.

- *Eliminate suspect(s) or focus further on suspect(s).*

Protocols must be in place for organized, efficient, and thorough fact-finding, specific information evaluation, and assessment—then accurate and complete case documentation.

The utility of consent is huge, and so is the Constitutional responsibility of investigators to comply with the fourth amendment standards:

- Voluntariness

- Scope

- Third-party concerns

Investigators know that the most important objectives in all homicide investigations are identifying, collecting, analyzing, and processing information quickly and effectively and then acting just as efficiently on that data to achieve maximum results.

The effectiveness of the investigation often depends on the investigative team's ability to quickly process and complete prioritized leads to swiftly provide answers to the case agent. Uncovering information that establishes clues and generates leads that tailor the focus and scope of the investigative effort is a critical issue.

Further, investigative teams must be able to locate and interview people quickly to lock individuals into statements to provide the maximum indicia of credibility and reliability; locate and preserve valuable evidence; and obtain and document the most accurate observations and accounts, putting together specific timelines. Investigators should use "the fact-finding capsule," a fundamental method illustrated by several investigative tactics completed under three important rules:

- **Haste:** quickly accomplish all tasks to seize the initiative and promptly develop facts.

- **Specificity:** precisely explore all issues to obtain facts detailed enough to make objective judgments and correlations.

- **Element of surprise:** prevent interviewees from getting their stories together and deter the interjection of attorneys into an efficient interview process.

The tactical steps of a homicide investigation should include a specific interview, a timeline documenting the witness's or suspect's physical location, what happened at those places over a time period necessary and germane to the case, and a well-documented statement.

If the suspect articulates an alibi, investigators immediately should conduct follow-up verification interviews, observing, inspecting, and documenting the suspect's shoes, clothing, and physical appearance, as well as any premises and personal effects involved.

These basic investigatory steps remain critical in the homicide investigation to eliminate or focus upon individuals as suspects. The framework provided by the fact-finding capsule covers the bases in an expedient and thorough manner, leaving no stone unturned. Information gleaned from this concept is then used in later briefings to corroborate or dispel other information produced through the investigative process afoot.

The chief investigator acts as the central clearinghouse for all case information, from briefings and various reports throughout the day to other investigators sharing their findings. A key factor in this framework is the continuing communication and consultation with the lead investigator by other investigators utilizing this process. This is especially true before investigators take the initiative to go to other locations or interview additional witnesses derived from their interview. The reason the chief investigator needs to be contacted and kept in the loop has two main points:

- To ensure that investigative actions are in line with orderly case progression (serial order or priority) where victims, witnesses, or suspects are managed properly

- To ensure the investigators working in the field have the latest intelligence or case-specific information from the lead investigator.

This procedure develops a state of shared consciousness between every pertinent member of the investigative team. This team includes the investigators on the case, the ME, forensics technicians, and crime laboratory scientists such as firearms examiners and serologists.

The investigative team must not be just a *team* but be a coherent *teaming* group.[60]

When the work requires people to juggle multiple objectives with minimal oversight, people must be able to shift from one situation to another while maintaining high levels of communication and tight coordination. This is when it is very helpful to integrate perspectives from different disciplines in the progression of the investigation.

When collaborating across the various or dispersed disciplines or locations, sometimes preplanned coordination is impossible or unrealistic due to the time pressures or changing nature of the work. Complex information must be processed, synthesized, and put to good use quickly through ongoing and constant communication. Strong connectivity and in-depth systematic understanding among partners in the case is critically important and time sensitive. These collaborations are conducive to quicker and more accurate interpretations of facts and evidence and improved strategic decisions within the investigation. Homicide cases define the importance of the practice of teaming.

Circumstances may arise under the fact-finding capsule circumstances where question stains, firearms, ammunition, hairs, and fibers all need priority examination for elimination or the inclusion as evidence in the case to highlight the path forward. Search and seizure questions or scenarios may need to be supported by advice from the prosecutor to provide sound legal grounding. Autopsy information may become critical in the corroboration of a suspect's or witness's statement. The ME needs to know the scene; the investigator needs to know autopsy results; the crime scene technician or

---

60 A. C. Edmondson, *Teaming: How Organizations Learn, Innovate, and Compete in the Knowledge Economy* (City of Publication: Hoboken NJ. John Wiley & Sons, 2012).

specialist needs to share facts with both the ME and the investigator. The informational products from the roles and responsibilities of all must be in a common informational space for all. The common goal is a partnership together toward understanding, sense-making, and proactive information for sharing and support.

Investigators in the homicide unit should receive annual training regarding the crime lab's capabilities.[61] A detective, or team of detectives, with complete oversight of the case must liaise with multiple forensic experts to determine the most appropriate analysis tactic for each piece of evidence. This creates temporal and physical delays in the parsing of information to and from experts with each passage of information standing the chance of loss or oversight. It is also notable that no lines of communication typically exist between experts, who regularly operate in silos. Investigators must promote an ongoing, constant stream of intelligence between and across experts and investigators as the case progresses. This allows ongoing, real-time support to the investigation.

An advantage in the ability to solve cases within the context of the fact-finding capsule is knowing the value and continuing utility of the consensual search. Knowing what to look for, examine, and collect during a consent to search, whether premises, vehicle, or person, is important. Suspect statements regarding those searches are also important to document for follow-up investigation.

---

61   B. Hapman, D. Keatley, G. Oatley, J. Coumbaros, and G. Maker, "A Review and Recommendations for the Integration of Forensic Expertise within Police Cold Case Reviews," *Journal of Criminal Psychology* 10, no. 2 (2020): 79–91.

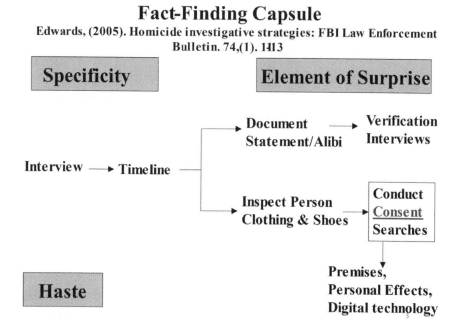

Fact-Finding Capsule

Edwards, (2005). Homicide investigative strategies: FBI Law Enforcement Bulletin. 74,(1). 1113

The advent of technologies and modern communications creates a need to apply these old strategies in a new fashion. In today's world, almost every household has access to or possession of computers, and most individuals possess cell phones. Every technological asset, whether at home or work, has records, communications, tolls, or billings that may reveal valuable evidence regarding a person's lifestyle, friends, associates, enemies, or businesses.

This information quickly can identify motives and other articulative facts essential to determining an individual's victimology or suspectology. Learning these details during traditional interviews proves essential to the investigative effort.

Absent exigent circumstances, the Fourth Amendment applies to the protection of these technologies and most records derived from their utility. Therefore, investigators oftentimes need consent or search warrants to develop the information. Investigators know that they must obtain preservation orders and immediately address all issues in an ongoing investigation. A common theme in this book is the first forty-eight hours may prove critical, leading to the prompt investigative trilogy's importance as a homicide investigator's utility as a framework.

The prompt investigative trilogy has three particular areas:

1. Specific focus (immediate)

2. General coverage (immediate)

3. Informative (pending)

Teams of investigators need to be *dedicated separately* to each area simultaneously during the investigation and direct information from all three areas to the central clearinghouse (i.e., the lead investigator, case agent, or detective in the case). At that time, teams should process information, form theories, and take steps regarding the focus, scope, and need for additional resources.

Specific focus witnesses: Evidence, events, and facts make up the specific focus. These categories apply to those issues immediately identified at the inception of the investigation. For instance, at a crime scene, certain witnesses may have been present at the time of the crime. Responding officers often identify suspects based upon initial witness information regarding relationships or motives. Distinctive pieces of evidence may be in plain view, and events or facts may exist that investigators must address: Items found on or around the victim. Circumstances regarding recent contacts or association with the victim. These immediately apparent issues demand specific focus, whether in crime-scene processing or interviews.

General coverage: While teams of investigators address those specific focus issues, a second team should handle the general coverage issue, which comprises four areas.

First, they should conduct neighborhood canvasses, which deals with people in close vicinity to others, and make observations or assessments regarding the situational environmental issues in connection with proximity.

In contemporary times, people need to be interviewed in canvass-type operations to be "locked in" to their truthful story while it is fresh on their minds. These interviews are time sensitive and must be conducted early. This proactive measure may prevent the opportunity for a potential witness, or an agenda-driven person, to create a new unknown and undocumented narrative later. Sometimes people living or located in a geographic area at the time of the crime will be solicited from other agenda-driven individuals to corroborate an alternate story—for example, the influences on people by social media, earned media, or other groups of people regarding their assumptions of the facts in the case. Investigators should never be surprised by an individual who was at a scene or in the proximity to the scene that has provided their observations to those other than officers involved in the investigation.

Second, interviews of friends, families, and associates may determine victimology or suspectology information while such information is fresh and untainted by the direction of the investigation.

Third, coworkers or employers may provide other information regarding victims and suspects.

Finally, construction of definite victim/suspect timelines should outline the environment, proximity, locations, and times.

The informative: This aspect was created by modern technologies. Just as an inventory of a person's residence after a homicide provides many facts about that individual, so does the information from the numerous technologies available today. This area consists of records from video sources like CCTV, social media, cell phones, GPS, cyber relationships, and information spaces. This also includes the computer hard drives (e.g., laptops, notebooks, desktops, and servers), diaries, notes, and documents. "Informative" includes data that persons of interest in the investigation use in their lives, interest, travels, interactions with others, and geographic connections: Stingray technology for cell location and information. Obtaining the necessary search warrants for cell phone data. Geofencing is one such technology at this stage where officers apply for a warrant to define an area of interest and a time period to identify suspects.

This team is also important for inventorying camera footage or other digital investigation to keep the other two teams on the streets fact-finding.

Note: A preservation letter should be sent to the provider via email or fax as soon as possible to preserve records before they are discarded and cannot be recovered. This is particularly an issue with text message and voice mail content, which are generally retained for only seventy-two hours.

The preservation letter freezes information, secures its retention, and provides the investigator time to apply for a search warrant. Its hierarchy of protection may include transactional records (name, number, billing records, etc.), numbers dialed from or to a phone, or content from stored communication (email, voice mail, text messages, etc.)

All investigations should have a three-phase strategy:

First, investigators should ensure the availability of proper resources to conduct the investigation in the most efficient and competent manner to stabilize and organize the effort to gather all facts.

Second, teams quickly should educate all investigators with as much information as possible.

Third, investigators expeditiously should investigate the case, establishing focus early. More often than not, the focus of the investigation (the result of the information gathered and the interpretation of that data) will determine its success.

Contemporary times demand investigators simultaneously accomplish multiple tasks and quickly analyze information to seize the initiative and react timely and accurately to any given scenario. The fact-finding capsule, complemented by the prompt investigative trilogy, represents the necessary formula to factor into the equation regarding investigatory demands associated with homicide cases. These protocols will ensure the most efficient use of time in connection with the gathering of facts and seizing of evidence.

Investigations are both time sensitive and information sensitive. Time is a nonrenewable resource tethered to the ability to seize the initiative and/or capture deteriorating information, recollections, and tangible evidence. The more effective and efficient the investigation can become without compromising the case quality and professional obligations the better it's outcomes and results.

The concept of the prompt investigative trilogy is designed to improve both time and information management. As a result, three different and important perspectives are blended into one vessel of global information in the case. The chief investigator can then use this vessel to pour information into a common pool of knowledge at the investigative briefing, where all investigators learn and share their views in the mosaicking environment created within the investigation.

THE PROMPT INVESTIGATIVE TRILOGY

Edwards, "Homicide Investigative Strategies," *FBI Law Enforcement Bulletin* 74, no. 1 (2005): 11–13.

IMMEDIATE SPECIFIC FOCUS	IMMEDIATE GENERAL COVERAGE	PENDING INFORMATIVE
Specific witnesses identified from the scene	Neighborhood canvass	Cell phone locations and records
Specific evidence at scene or nexus to the victim/suspect	Friends, family, and associates interviews	Computer hard drives, SSDs, other digital and cloud storage technologies
Specific events learned before, during, or after the incident	Coworkers' interviews	CCTV, geofencing, other location-specific technologies
Specific facts from the case that require an exigent response	Specific timelines that capture behavior and activities	Social media content (past and present), active monitoring

The Structure, Process, and Functions

The next illustration takes in all of the components and places them in a framework where we can organize and manage the homicide case effectively. The roles and responsibilities are married to open and ongoing lines of communication in support of each member of the investigative team and forensic effort.

This investigative effort involves all the different components working seamlessly in sync and in harmony toward common goals and specific expectations under an umbrella of understood policy and procedural standards within the context of the investigative realities in the case.

Notice that the chief investigating officer serves as the central clearinghouse for all information and approves investigative strategies and actions in the case. All investigators and support staff must keep the chief investigator informed. Supervisors, support staff, and the intelligence component are attached to support the role and responsibility of the chief investigator. This role emphasizes why the chief investigator must be a communications director and conduit to keep all informed.

The below illustrates the proper coordination and open lines of ongoing communications between all of the different domains of responsibility and how they collectively come together to advance the investigation in a structured and meaningful manner.

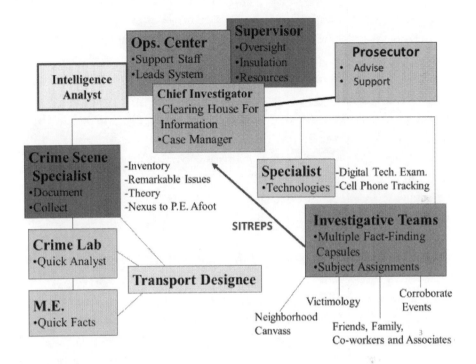

Case Studies Illustrating These Concepts:

Fact-Finding Capsule

The body of a young man was found dumped in a ditch beside a dirt road. He had been stabbed multiple times. The investigation revealed that he was a known cocaine street dealer in the community. Interviews identified many prior customers. A police informer identified a particular customer who was addicted and had been a regular of the victim's.

This suspect was approached at his home by agents. At the initial interview, the suspect provided an alibi to the agents. The agents believed the suspect was being deceptive. His story was relayed to other agents by radio for follow-up to verify or disprove the alibi.

In the interim, agents noticed the suspect's tennis shoes were wet. It had not been raining, and the suspect stated he had recently washed his shoes. The suspect gave his consent in response to the agents' request for his person, premises, and vehicle.

Agents found the remnants of red dirt in the crevices of the tread on the bottom of his shoes. A red stain was found on the white cloth inner pockets of his blue jeans. Agents found that his pickup truck interior had been washed and had not dried completely. A search of the threshold of the passenger door revealed bloodstains in the crevice of the plastic.

It was later determined that the suspect had lied about his whereabouts around the time of the victim's death. The statements in combination with the evidence discovery led to an admission by the suspect for the crime. Later lab results linked the victim to the stains discovered on the victim's properties and collected by the agents.

Prompt Investigative Trilogy

A young married woman became involved with an unmarried man in a passionate sexual affair. She wanted out of her marriage and solicited the clandestine boyfriend to help murder her husband. She left the door open one night, and the boyfriend covertly entered the home, beat the husband in his sleep with a pipe, and then cut his throat.

Together the illicit couple worked to stage a home invasion at the scene, and when the boyfriend was clear, the wife of the victim called 911 in the middle of the night to report the crime.

On arrival it was clear from the staged broken glass at the back door windowpane to the arrangement of property on the floor that the scene had probably been staged. The victim's pickup truck had been stolen from the scene. The investigative team met to discern leads and follow up. One team was dedicated to the crime scene and witnesses linked to it. A second team collected the cell phones to conduct forensic examinations of its context. A third team started neighborhood canvassing.

The wife gave an emotional statement as to her whereabouts during the crime. She claimed she had been asleep in bed lying beside her husband when the perpetrators entered the room and started beating her husband. She claimed she had been held at knifepoint and carried to the den, where she had been forced to empty her purse. She stated that the invaders stole her money and left. She stated that she went back to the bedroom, and her husband was found dead.

The statement added to the agents' beliefs regarding the scene being staged because the crime scene now told a different story from the now suspect wife. Her story about being in the bed beside her husband was false. The tremendous amount of blood spatter in the bedroom covered the sheets all over the bed and around the location the husband had been beaten. If the woman's story were true, there would have been blood spatter voids on the sheets where she claims she was lying and bloodstains on her clothing. This evidence caused the agents to focus on her as a suspect.

After about six hours, the case agent called a briefing where mosaicking occurred with reports from the different teams. The digital technologies team reported texts were found on the suspect wife's phone that identified a secret love affair and revealed the identity and phone information of the romantic partner, who had become a suspect due his many overt texts outlining his surveillance of the victim and an earlier attempt where the male suspect tried to kill the victim alone that had failed when neighbors spotted him. The cell number of the male suspect was tracked and placed the male suspect at the wife's school, where she'd worked the day before the murder, and at the crime scene the night of the murder. Further, the cell phone tower locations led agents to a nearby county, where they located the victim's truck at a bar, where the owner of the bar identified the wife's boyfriend with the stolen truck.

The neighborhood canvass team reported that they had interviewed a neighbor who lived less than a mile from the victim's residence and knew him well. The neighbor advised he was riding by three days ago and saw a man sitting in his car beside the road across the yard from the victim's residence. The neighbor said he approached the suspected prowler and found that he had no good reason to be where he was located. The neighbor provided a description that matched the suspect boyfriend and independently corroborated a text from three days earlier on the suspect wife's phone about the first murder attempt being spoiled.

The information that was simultaneously collected and the mosaicking that occurred at the investigator's briefing placed the chief investigator in an outstanding position to shift the interview of the wife to an interrogation. When the investigator showed the wife the evidence incriminating her and her boyfriend, she confessed and made statements and implicated her boyfriend in the murder.

Both the wife and boyfriend were convicted of murder.

Central to this case study is the effectiveness of the three different teams working independently from each other while simultaneously working with each other toward a common investigative goal, then the benefit of these teams coming together to share and compare the myriad of facts and circumstances connected to the case.

Time is saved, information is expedited, and the chief investigator is placed in a better position for sense-making and case-theory development. Such develops important leads and results in sound positions to draw conclusions grounded in specific facts and credible evidence.

Search Warrants in Homicide Cases

Paula K. Smith, in her 2006 argument[62] in front of the US Supreme Court in the case of *Georgia v. Randolph*, stated an investigator(s) charge in a meaningful manner: "We measure what is reasonable on the part of the Police by looking at what they know."

- Ensure the rule of law is followed and the warrant is based in probable cause to believe that the particular items will be in the particular place, at this particular time.

- Follow the rule of specificity in all warrants.

- Make reasonable inferences (articulate the specific facts that draw a nexus to the particular items sought and their relationship to the totality of facts and circumstances in the case. The key is to demonstrate objective reasons to support logical inferences why particular evidence would be located at a particular place).

---

62   Georgia v Randolph, 547 U.S. (2006).

- Seek to particularly describe all items (exact description of instrumentalities is a virtual impossibility; the searching officer can only be expected to describe the generic class of the items they are seeking).

- Document plain-view events and their nexus for examinations of materials as evidence

- Seek additional authority and amend warrant to extend scope if necessary.

Staleness of Information
Articulation of reasonable inferences and nexus to evidence...

- Conditions described in the affidavit might yet prevail at the time of the issuance of the warrant.

- Time is assuredly an element of the concept of probable cause.

- Staleness is measured in found in "reason" not in "case law"; below are examples of valid concepts:

  – Disposable versus of continuing utility to the suspect

  – Perishable versus nonperishable evidence sought

  – A one-time event versus ongoing behavior, conduct, or scheme

Search warrants often become a critical asset to the homicide investigators in the progression of their case. Such illustrates why investigators must have the acumen required to frame and craft search warrant affidavits that enable the investigator to enhance their ability to find evidence in a case.

Case Study regarding Search Warrants

The text from the record of a Georgia Supreme Court case illustrates an excellent example regarding staleness in case facts regarding a homicide case.[63]

In her statement, she said that she was in the apartment when Lejeune shot Ronnie Davis in the head, that she heard the shot and saw Lejeune holding the gun, and that he told her he had done it. Lejeune cut up the body, staining the carpet with blood, and they placed the body parts in Lejeune's Toyota Corolla.

They drove to the cemetery and burned the body parts, but they kept the head because the bullet was still inside it. They took the head to Lejeune's parents' house on Lake Lanier, where Lejeune placed it in a basement vise and tried to extract the bullet. He was unsuccessful, so he placed the head in a bucket, poured cement into it, and dumped it in Lake Lanier. Some of Anand's statement corroborated information provided by Kenneth Vaughn, a previous informant in the case, and information obtained through a "controlled call," wherein the police overheard her and Lejeune before their arrest make incriminating comments about cleaning blood out of the apartment carpet.

The state gave Anand's statement and the case file, with all the evidence and information pertaining to the suppressed searches redacted out, to GBI Special Agent Lang, who was uninvolved in the previous investigation of the case.

Agent Lang was generally aware that prior searches in the case had been suppressed, but he was not told about any evidence that had been seized or where he should look. Agent Lang believed that blood evidence might still be present in the apartment and the car trunk because blood evidence does not degrade when protected from the elements.

Similarly, he believed that some blood and tissue from the victim's head might have transferred to the vise grip and might still be present on the vise and basement floor in Lejeune's parents' house.

He consulted with a blood expert, Dr. Henry Lee, who supported this theory. In May 2003, he obtained supporting affidavits, actually written

---

63 *Lejeune v. the State*, 276 Ga. 179 (2003).

by another GBI agent, and sought search warrants from judicial officers in Fulton County (for the apartment), DeKalb County (for the car), and Hall County (for Lejeune's parents' house). The search warrants were granted, and blood evidence was obtained from all three locations.

Lejeune moved to suppress the results of this search, alleging that the information about the vise was stale because there was no information provided in the affidavit that indicated that the vise would still be there after five years. The trial court found probable cause for the police to search the house for blood, and it denied the motion to suppress the blood evidence found in the parents' basement. However, it granted Lejeune's motion to suppress the vise and blood evidence found on the vise because the information contained in the affidavit about the vise was stale.

The state appealed this ruling.

Because there was probable cause to authorize the search for blood evidence in the house, the police were legally permitted to be inside the basement and reasonably permitted to look on surfaces where blood might be located, including the vise. Any blood evidence uncovered as a result of the swabbing of the vise is admissible. We also conclude that the information about the vise contained in the supporting affidavit for the search warrant was not stale.

The ultimate criterion in determining the degree of evaporation of probable cause is not case law but reason. The likelihood that the evidence sought is still in place is a function not simply of watch and calendar but of variables that do not punch a clock: the character of the crime, of the criminal, of the thing to be seized (perishable and easily transferable or of enduring utility to its holder?), of the place to be searched (mere criminal forum of convenience or secure operational base?), etc. The observation of a half-smoked marijuana cigarette in an ashtray at a cocktail party may well be stale the day after the cleaning lady has been in; the observation of the burial of a corpse in a cellar may well not be stale three decades later.

A vise is not perishable or consumable, and it is of continuing utility to the owner. It is generally affixed to a workbench or table, and its placement is usually intended to be permanent. The owners of the house had not changed in the five years since Anand claimed that the vise had been used, and it was not unreasonable to expect the vise to still be there. It is the task of a reviewing court to simply "ensure that the magistrate had a 'substantial basis for concluding that probable cause existed and, contrary to the trial court's finding, the evidence showed that the magistrate had a substantial basis for concluding that the vise would still be in the house.'"

Therefore, the search warrant properly authorized the seizure of the vise, which is admissible at trial.

The Tremendous Importance of Statements in the Fact-Finding Process

- Provides valuable witness accounts/stories

- Leads to evidence discovery

- The independent corroboration and nexus to other statements that provide evidence

- Identifies those culpable or exonerates those innocent

- Historically will provide the means to prosecute for the cover-up when you can't prove the initial act...because people tend to lie to cover up rather than hold themselves accountable

- Leads to admissions and confessions of guilt

Statement Strategy

The chief investigator shapes the strategy and develops the tactical course regarding the type of interview course selected. Depending on the facts of the case and what is known or unknown, the investigator may choose to conduct an open-ended non accusatory interview to fact-find or lock the suspect into a lie for later utility in the investigation or cross-examination by the prosecutor at trial.

Often, even with enough probable cause to arrest the suspect, investigators may determine to conduct a noncustodial interview instead of custodial. Three avenues are generally taken in these strategies:

- General fact-finding: open-ended questions

- Dual-strategy focus: acquiescence to the suspect's lie stream (to lock them into their lie) until such time to challenge of lie stream of the suspect directly

- Wedge utility: going after admissions by showing the suspect evidence

Noncustodial Fishing

- Lies are your ally.

- Lock them in and tie them down to specific facts and circumstances.

- Produce timelines.

- Develop counterstatement evidence (create wedges) for the additional interviews or later custodial interview.

In-Custody Interviews

Following *Jackson-Denno 378 U.S. 1964*, in-custody interviews require the following:

- Miranda and waiver of rights

- Voluntariness

- No coercion

- No hope or benefit of reward

Research-Based Interview Models

- **Cognitive behavior interview protocols**: includes a number of memory-enhancing techniques (e.g., adapting questions to the interviewee's unique perspective and mentally reinstating the context of the original event) and elements related to the social dynamics of the interview setting (e.g., building rapport).

  - *Focuses mostly on nonaccusatory fact-finding interviews*

- **Strategic use of evidence (SUE) technique:** an interviewing framework that aims to improve the ability to make correct judgments of credibility, through the elicitation of cues to deception and truth

- **PEACE model:** preparation and planning, engage and explain, account, closure, and evaluate

- **The REID interview technique:** three components—factual analysis, interview, and interrogation

Whatever model is used or combinations, the investigator should plan their interview. The initial contact, pertinent questions, evidence inventories, and context of the interviews need a framework of planning grounded in forethought regarding the case information nexus to the interviewee (victim, witness, suspect).

The REID interview technique has three connected stages for progression forward. First is the factual analysis. Second is the interview, and third is the interrogation. Each stage develops the foundation for the next stage to be used and progresses forward with a planned and structured interview.

The PEACE model has five stages of interviewing: planning and preparation, engage and explain, account, closure, and evaluation. Each of the five stages contains specific behaviors that are thought to be required for a successful interview.

The investigator's planning can shape and mold the forecast of the interview based on the factual analysis of the case. The factual analysis is when the investigator gathers the facts of the case regarding suspects, victims, witnesses, crime scene, type of crime, and relevant evidence. That information can be used to analyze and categorize each of them to form the dependent and independent evidence. Dependent evidence is evidence that is known to police and the suspect only. Another term for *dependent evidence* is *hold-back evidence*. Independent evidence is the evidence that is known only to the suspect and is sought out by the police. The facts are divided into dependent and independent evidence. This forms the list of questions that an investigator would be asking of a suspect in an interview or an interrogation.[64]

The working-environment norms of police investigators were found to be strongly associated with planning intentions. Also, investigators' self-efficacy of their planning-related capabilities was also found to have a strong relationship with intention and *perceived level of planning*. Above all, intention to plan was found to have a powerful association with interview planning. Contrary to common beliefs regarding possible reasons for poor planning (i.e., time pressure), the present study found that investigators' own perception of their planning skills and their subjective norms appeared to potentially play a more substantial role.[65]

The SUE technique is an interviewing framework that aims to improve the ability to make correct judgments of credibility, through the elicitation of cues to deception and truth.[66] The SUE technique consists of a theoretical level of reasoning regarding the state of mind in which liars and truth-tellers approach an interview.

---

64 J. A. Holmgren, *Interviewing and Interrogation: A Canadian Critical and Practical Perspective* (Ontario, Canada: Nelson Education, 2017).

65 J. Kim, D. Walsh, R. Bull, and H. Bergstrøm, "Planning Ahead? An Exploratory Study of South Korean Investigators' Beliefs about Their Planning for Investigative Interviews of Suspects," *Journal of Police and Criminal Psychology* 33, no. 2 (2018): 158–174.

66 M. Hartwig, P. A. Granhag, and T. Luke, "Strategic Use of Evidence during Investigative Interviews: The State of the Science," *Credibility Assessment* (2014): 1–36.

This theoretical level is anchored in foundational social cognitive theories of self-regulatory behavior. The theoretical reasoning translates into predictions about different counterinterrogation strategies employed by liars and truth-tellers, which in turn translate into predictions about different patterns of verbal behavior during an interview.

The SUE technique also consists of a number of specific, concrete tactics for how to structure, plan, and pose questions in order to produce cues to deception in the form of discrepancies with facts (i.e., statement–evidence inconsistencies). Further, the technique offers recommendations for when and how to disclose the relevant information in order to produce revisions in deceptive subjects' accounts (i.e., within-statement inconsistencies). Thus, the SUE framework provides useful practical tools for interviewers and also strengthens researchers' theoretical understanding of the behavior of interviewees.

Important Operational Concerns regarding Interviews

The interview technique used by the investigator or synthesis of techniques must be legally sound, factually focused, and strategically planned. Investigators must know the evidence in the case and understand the in-depth insight into the existing fact patterns, crime scene, and autopsy (or at least facts regarding wounds or trauma).

Investigators should never bluff a suspect unless they know for certain that such a bluff cannot be compromised by known facts available to the suspect. The ability to show the suspect irrefutable evidence against the suspect often serves as a catalyst toward an admission of guilt. Minimization and plays on the conscience may also be effective. Caution should be used with any language that may be deemed as coercive or hints toward a hope, benefit, or reward that could render the statement involuntary and inadmissible. Remember the law and the in-depth rules from Jackson-Denno hearings regarding admissions.

Many times, statements that lack the appropriate degree of specificity are open to many interpretations. Statements must be used to corner or "lock" people into a solid position where the objective, specific facts defeat subjective interpretation or opinion. A lie is difficult to prove without first locking the person into their specific account and then eliminating all "wiggle room." After one is locked into a statement or account, then you must identify and prove each component of the lie. Work by design to eliminate every other reasonable hypothesis but the lie.

In many cases, the utility of prior inconsistent statements or provable narratives where a suspect has lied have considerable influence upon a jury's determination of guilt.

Reinterviews / Second Statements

- **Concern:** continuity of experience calls for the same investigator as the first time (unless other circumstances deem differently).

- **Close case coordination with lead investigator** to review the story told for credibility or the need for additional follow-up leads to establish or refute an alibi.

- **If targeted toward deception:** the facts must defeat the subject's word to the degree necessary to prove the lie.

- **Documented properly:** audio/video (covert or overt if your state law applies).

Timelines Can Be Beneficial

Timelines create a mental picture of activities and movements between locations and specific interactions with people. It may open windows into new insights when compared with or to other witnesses, victims, or suspects.

- Creates a *visual* chronological history of movements, locations, and events of the suspect, victim, or witness

- Determines the contact and proximity of suspect to a victim or a particular scene

- Captures the relationship between time, activity, incidents, circumstances, and environment within the statement provided

- Captures the many logical sequences to test and measure against other information from the investigation

- Take proactive measures to identify Brady issues early on in the case

- Develops opportunities to corroborate information points

- Creates a visual reconstruction and means to correlate (comparison and contrast)

- Prepares the investigator and prosecutor for courtroom testimony

- Acts as demonstrative evidence in grand jury or at trial

The investigator can thoroughly read the statements provided and draw out a timeline by hand or digitally. A preferred practice is that the timeline is constructed and developed by both the interviewee and the investigator during their session, then reviewed and proofread together to ensure accuracy.

Investigators must ensure they document their statements appropriately and cover all the bases.

- Application required (video, audio, or written)

- All elements of the crime included in the four corners of the statements

- Specific and thoroughly taken, leaving no stone unturned

- Tested facts by specific questions or detailed responses

- Examined for areas that require independent corroboration

- No Bruton rule problems where codefendants' statements against each other are relied upon (the codefendant must testify and be available for cross-examination per the right of confrontation at court)

- Vetted for follow-up lead generation

Lead Investigator's Review of Statements

- Provides case-specific knowledge

- Comparison and contrast with other statements

- Test for thoroughness, accuracy, and completeness

  - Degree of specificity

  - Culpability or exculpatory (Brady issues)

  - Consistency or inconsistency with all other evidence and statements

  - Independent corroboration or lack thereof

  - Reinterview if required (something left out or new information)

  - Follow-up leads

Informants can be beneficial or cause tremendous problems in homicide cases.

The key to credible information from the use of informants is informant management by the investigator. Informants by their very nature bring forth tremendous issues, potential for case failure, and a demand for specific management by investigators and oversight by supervisors. Informant credibility always comes into question. Their background and association with defendants and police will be questioned. Remember, informants with criminal convictions may become impeachable witnesses.

Informants must be interviewed in specific, skeptical, probing, challenging, and in-depth terms.

All must be uncovered regarding their history, background, status, motives, intentions, designs, and conduct. All must be thoroughly documented.

Investigators must never make promises, deals, or agreements with informants absent direct involvement, approval, and documentation by the prosecutor in the case.

Informant cause problems in homicide investigations when they

- provide false or misleading information,

- are convicted felons that are impeachable witnesses in court,

- use their status for their own purposes,

- have hidden agendas or ulterior motives,

- are involved in criminal activity or improper conduct at the same time,

- allege that promises/deals were made by police in return for their cooperation, or

- are in-custody informants (inmates and convicts).

Caution with In-Custody Witnesses/Informants

In-custody informants / witness inmates require very special attention. Because of their situation, experiences, and motives, they present a huge but manageable risk. An extensive and thorough examination of their credibility and reliability must performed. Their information must be carefully evaluated and tested.

The below list can be incorporated into the investigative process to minimize risk with statements from inmates:

- Evaluate An evaluation of the informant/inmate basis of knowledge (underlying circumstances and how they know what they claim to know)

- Assess the inmate sources opportunity to hear, see, or know what they say they know ensure they can articulate the underlying circumstances regarding how they received their information

- Seek independent corroboration from other sources

- Probe the specifics and details contained within the statements and evaluate the degree of access the informant had to the sources

- Analyze all statements or discoveries of evidence from the inmate information that could only be known by the perpetrator of the crime

- The degree of access the inmate/informant had to other witnesses, police officers, and media

- Any prior or inconsistent statements made by the inmate

- Any motives, agreements, benefits, hopes, concerns, fears, or dangers

- Past inmate background and records

- Past inmates as cellmates or in the same institution who have a nexus to the case

- Mental state and mental history of the inmate

- Medical state and history of the inmate

- The manner/method in which the informant inmate was discovered, solicited, or came forward

- Their overall behavior and projected demeanor

- The effect of prolonged specific and thorough questioning of the inmate

- Other law enforcement contacts, visits, or interviews and the potential influence from those contacts

- Polygraph results

Covert Wires or the Informant/Conspirator Undercover Digital Recording of Suspects

There are times when the opportunity arises to develop additional evidence regarding a suspect's culpability by the covert recording of suspect statements by a witness, informant, or coconspirator in the case.

Great care and extraordinary effort should be placed in the very thorough debriefing of the informer wearing the device, including an in-depth examination to determine the nature of the informer's relationship with the suspect and whether it has changed over time. Moreover, an evaluation of the overall context of case and the weight of the evidence in hand needs to be examined in a thoughtful manner. The object of any investigative act (covert or overt) is to uncover and find the truth. Degrees of facts and evidence already obtained against a suspect or lack thereof may play a significant role in determining the context of an undercover meeting. Is the meeting a fact-finding mission or opportunity to obtain additional evidence on a known offender? The answer to this question will result in making informed decisions regarding investigative strategy. The risk of the suspect exploiting their position by telling lies that must be revealed later as exculpatory statements must be weighed as well.

The informer's meeting location, initiation of conversation, manner, and substance must be legal, targeted to finding the truth, structured, and well planned.

Poor judgments occur due to lack of attention, case pressure, or making exceptions to existing policy and procedure. There are four other technical areas of concern to be evaluated and covered:

- Safety

- Legal considerations

- Environment (beware of music or other loud noise that would impede recordings)

- Technical concerns with batteries, antenna, connections (cell signal, internet, RF)

The Utility of the Polygraph Diagnostic and Interrogatory

The polygraph is a very helpful tool in investigation. It can be effective at creating an environment and atmosphere for obtaining admissions or confessions. It can generate leads for important follow-up. It can also be meaningful in combination with other exculpatory facts and circumstances to exonerate a suspect. In cases with multiple suspects or uncooperative witnesses, the polygraph can be the lever to open up the floodgates to the truth by creating a condition to transform a deceptive person into a truthful one. The polygraph can test the truth (diagnostics) or find the truth (interrogatory) in the context of case theory.

- Diagnostics works toward the ultimate goal of determining whether the statements are based upon truth or a deception.

- Interrogatory seeks to find the truth through the use of the polygraph as a tool in the interview and to gain admissible admissions or confessions of the crime or violation investigated.

The reliability of the polygraph should not become an issue. It should be viewed and used as an investigative tool only. To ensure it benefits the investigation, investigators must work in close concert with the polygraph examiner to provide in-depth case facts and context, so the examiner is educated enough regarding the case to form specific questions for the witness or suspect to be ask.

Polygraph Operations
Reliability versus utility:

- Many suspects provide admissions in the pretest phase of the polygraph examination

- The polygraph may be a useful tool in the process of elimination of suspects or credibility of witnesses

- The polygraph is an excellent tool to obtain voluntary statements

- The very nature of a polygraph exam may identify important issues and generate suspect motivations to talk

- The polygraphs function as a tool may provide the investigator a reliable understanding of who may or may not be involved in the death

Ensure Premeetings with Polygraph Examinator

- The investigator must Thoroughly brief the polygraph examiner regarding the specific facts of the case

- The investigator must work in concert with the polygraph examiner to develop narrowly tailored and very specific questions within the context of the criminal act

- The investigator should ensure that the examinee/suspect is told to not use any illegal drugs and rest before the polygraph, preferably overnight in a normal sleep cycle (it should be noted that prescription drugs that are controlled substances may also adversely affect the polygraph test)

GBI agent Chuck Sullenger, an outstanding veteran homicide investigator, now polygraph examiner, once provided this informative advice:

"It is critical that the specific questions to be asked are covered in an interview with the examinee prior to the polygraph by the interviewing investigator. Questions such as, "Did you shoot John Doe?" and "Do you know for sure who shot John Doe?" and "Were you present [or did you participate] when John Doe was shot?" must never be heard first by the examinee from the examiner. The examinee should have already heard an entire array of very specific questions regarding his/her involvement in the death from the interviewing investigator prior to the introduction of the polygraph examiner. The innocent examinee must have time to overcome the shock of being asked those very specific and inculpatory questions and have resolved in their mind that they did not do that act. The brain's memory, in concert with the autonomic nervous system, will handle the guilty examinee, for they cannot "*unremember*" a clear memory to the specific questions."

Eyewitness Identification

Eyewitness identification remains a controversial area in criminal investigation. These operations must be done under a veil of caution with careful planning. Prosecutor involvement is also important.

Our supreme court provided five prime concerns in *Manson v. Braithwaite* years ago in 1977. Failure to comply often leads to misidentification.

- The degree of attention the eyewitness focused on the perpetrator

- The accuracy of the witness's description of the perpetrator

- The eyewitness's opportunity to view the perpetrator at the crime scene

- The time elapsed between the witness's identification of the suspect and witnessing the crime

- The certainty of the witness's identification of the suspect

Investigators need to take all five of these concerns into thoughtful consideration in every case that involves an eyewitness identification.

Potential Problems with Eyewitness Identification

- Witnesses are biased to recall their initial low-confidence IDs as having been made with high confidence.[67]

- People tend to recall the past in a way that is consistent with their current beliefs.[68]

---

67 G. L. Wells and A. L. Bradfield, "'Good, You Identified the Suspect': Feedback to Eyewitnesses Distorts Their Reports of the Witnessing Experience," *Journal of Applied Psychology* 83, no. 3 (1998): 360.

68 U. Hoffrage, R. Hertwig, and G. Gigerenzer, "Hindsight Bias: A By-Product of Knowledge Updating?," *Journal of Experimental Psychology: Learning, Memory, and Cognition*, 26, no. 3 (2000): 566.

- "Erroneous identification of the accused constitutes is the major cause of known wrongful convictions."

- "Mistaken eyewitness identification is particularly pronounced in a situation where the witness is a member of one race and the suspect is a member of another race."[69]

Show-ups, photo lineups, and physical lineups must be legally conducted, reasonable, and well documented.

Show-ups should always be timely and reasonable. They must be done in a well-planned and structural manner. Safety and proper witness presentation are critical elements.

The investigator must know their state's law regarding how much time has elapsed from the time of the incident to be legal under that particular state law and federal law.

Photo lineups and physical lineups must not be suggestive or administered improperly. Physical lineups need to be conducted in accordance with federal and state law with special attention to pre- or postformal charge status and the laws that apply.

Proper Eyewitness Identification Strategies[70]

- **The "double-blind" procedure / use of a blind administrator:** A "double-blind" lineup is one in which neither the administrator nor the eyewitness knows who the suspect is.

  - This prevents the administrator of the lineup from providing inadvertent or intentional verbal or nonverbal cues to influence the eyewitness to pick the suspect.

---

69   J. P. Wilson, K. Hugenberg, and M. J. Bernstein, "The Cross-Race Effect and Eyewitness Identification: How to Improve Recognition and Reduce Decision Errors in Eyewitness Situations," *Social Issues and Policy Review* 7, no. 1 (2013): 83–113.

70   https://innocenceproject.org/eyewitness-identification-reform/

- **Instructions:** "Instructions" are a series of statements issued by the lineup administrator to the eyewitness that deter the eyewitness from feeling compelled to make a selection.

    - They also prevent the eyewitness from looking to the lineup administrator for feedback during the identification procedure.

    - One of the recommended instructions includes the directive that *the suspect may or may not be present in the lineup.*

- **Composing the lineup:** Suspect photographs should be selected that do not bring unreasonable attention to the suspect.

    - Non suspect photographs or live lineup members (fillers) should be selected so that the suspect does not stand out from among the other fillers.

    - Law enforcement should select fillers using a blended approach that considers the fillers' resemblance to the description provided by the eyewitness and their resemblance to the police suspect.

- **Confidence statements:** Immediately following the lineup procedure, the eyewitness should provide a statement, in their own words, that articulates the level of confidence they have in the identification made.

- **The lineup procedure should be documented:** Ideally, the lineup procedure should be electronically recorded or photographed. If this is impracticable, an audio or written record should be made.[71]

---

71 G. L. Wells, M. Small, S. Penrod, R. S. Malpass, S. M. Fulero, and C. E. Brimacombe, "Eyewitness Identification Procedures: Recommendations for Lineups and Photospreads," *Law and Human Behavior*, 22, no. 6 (1998): 603.

Intelligence Function and Analyst Resources

Intelligence is a critical function in all criminal investigations. Agencies should develop intelligence-led policing programs to prevent, mitigate, and reduce crime.[72] Intelligence units are especially important in the context of gang murders. An analyst dedicated to the investigative team is very important toward the success of a homicide case. Intelligence analysts can save investigators valuable time and follow important leads from a laptop or phone. From driver's license records and criminal histories to the large array of open-source databases, intelligence analysts develop critical sources of background information and address exigent leads.

The chief investigator must ensure the analyst is well briefed and kept current as the investigation progresses. The intelligence function must have the resources to ensure data entry remains up to date and current. There needs to be a nexus between the analyst's function and the investigation's management of lead assignments and context. As always ongoing communication between the chief investigator and intelligence analyst is crucial in the successful progression of the case.

Leads Management

Investigations live and die on the efficient and effective process of identifying and assigning leads for fact-finding and sense-making in the case. The chief investigator looks at these leads in their totality with other known facts in the case to shape case theory and form investigative strategy. From this process, priorities are identified, and the sequential order of investigative actions are developed. Investigative leads provide case-specific information. From this information, other information is derived by follow-up leads. The chief investigator becomes the communications director. They are the librarian who files and retains information to share with other investigators, the ME, CSI, lab, or the prosecutor when they need to check out the results of previous information or a current assumption. The chief investigator is also responsible for the construction of a case file that contains narrative

---

72 J. B. Edwards, "Intelligence-Led Policing: Connecting Urban and Rural Operations," *FBI Law Enforcement Bulletin* 81 (2012): 19.

descriptions, statements, and detailed reports from the investigative actions during the course of the investigation. The leads-management system is a method to ensure oversight to ensure the paperwork (computerized reports) is completed.

Types of Leads-Management Systems

There are many different software applications for the capture and process of leads. Whatever system is selected, it must be simple and concise and not require much time to complete. It should serve as a pointer system not an in-depth database. The system will have a collateral and corollary utility as a database, but it should remain a part of a larger system or process to operate with speed and ease of use to investigators.

There are times where good leads-management systems involve sequential numbers and descriptions logged by the chief investigator in a notebook dedicated to leads progression and documentation. The simplest system should contain the following:

- Sequential numbers of leads as they are assigned

- Investigator's name to whom each lead is assigned

- Lead name

- Description of the lead

- Date provided to investigator

- Date lead completed by investigator

In my time at the GBI, our office designed a system we called "leads tracker." It used the Excel database to log and track leads and produce reports on the status of those leads, and it served as a case overview of the entire investigation.

The utility of a leads-management system will provide the "pictures" needed to enable the lead investigator to:

- keep up with leads out and leads in with additional follow-up assignments from a simple notebook to a computer program;

- know all issues in the investigation;

- maintain a road map/blueprint for the investigation efforts;

- determine resource allocation and needs;

- predict and forecast critical issues;

- choose strategies and tactics;

- direct, supervise, and coordinate the investigation as it unfolds; and

- correlate, compare, and analyze information.

Set Policies on How to Follow Up Leads and Be Consistent:

- Make any lead that might arguably tend to clear your suspect a priority.

- Consider developing a comprehensive questionnaire for things such as canvassing, phone interviews, tip investigation, elimination interviews for suspects, etc.

- Identify and deal with booger and monkey leads; they may become the basis of "reasonable doubt" during trial if they are not thoroughly investigated and eliminated up front.

- Ensure no "shortcutting" or failing to locate and interview subjects.

The leads-management system acts as a means to ensure that an assigned lead generates a specific report as to the result of that lead. The system holds investigators accountable to doing their paperwork in a timely manner. Thus, the chief investigator can manage their case file and comply with the prosecutor's responsibility for the discovery process with the court.

Intelligence units with analysts are an excellent resource, an important component to the investigation to the necessary team function. However, intelligence databases must be able to merge leads data from the system selected or have a separate function. Intelligence database entry takes too much time. A leads-management process is a pointer system. Its first and foremost mission is to provide a quick, efficient, and effective means for the chief investigating officer to

- gather, sort, and manage large amounts of information efficiently and effectively;

- assign and track leads in and leads out;

- document leads completed and leads pending;

- assign follow-up leads;

- ensure reports are completed later to cover the investigative action;

- manage overall focus, process, and progression of investigation; and

- manage the lead identification and lead in/out process cycle.

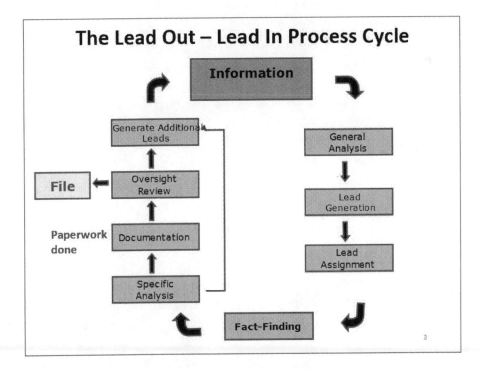

Investigative Summaries and Reports

The first seventy-two to ninety-six hours of the case many are running leads and reducing information to notes for later summaries, supplementals, or reports. The key is that official reports are completed in a timely matter and are accurate, thorough, and complete.

Individual summaries and reports need to meet the following criteria:[73]

- Professional, accurate, articulate, and complete are necessary elements of case-reporting documents.

- Reports must be specific and thorough.

- Officers must realize that administrative writings authored by them are official government documents.

- Officers are responsible for the documentation of all actions relevant to the investigation at all times.

- Officers should write what they mean and mean what they write.

- Officers are bound by that which is contained within the four corners of those documents that they author.

- Reports must reflect the details and issues necessary to support the officers' actions and judgments.

- Officers' reports are permanent records and reflect their abilities and the investigation's reputation.

Central to the case file process is supervisor oversight by a regular *collaborative* file review. This is when the supervisor reads the file in its full context, schedules a time, and sits down with the chief investigator to discuss leads,

---

73   SAC Ron Rohlfs, class regarding investigative summaries for GBI training, 1989.

follow-ups, and evidence. Grammar and spelling should also be checked to ensure professional products. From this process the file will have the appropriate oversight. Timeliness of this process should be set by policy with the latitude to adjust the process earlier if the type of case dictates such. Digital files will be problematic if the supervisor does not read the case summaries, statements, and evidence in context of the entire case.

Cold case investigation will often depend upon the overall performance of the investigator at the onset of the homicide.

These are examples that define why the quality of the original investigative processes and subsequent documentation is critical to cold case investigation:

- The overall quality of the investigator's documentation within the case file

- The degree of specificity within reports, statements, and interviews

- Lead identification and follow-up

- Timelines and victimology

- Suspect identification and elimination facts

- The processing, care, and storage of evidence (for examination and forensic application)

- Photographs, sketches, and documentation of the crime scene(s)

- Completeness and security of the case file

- Witness identification data

Often the passage of time leads to accidental loss of evidence or paper-work with cold case investigations. The loss or contamination of evidence is also a problem. Witnesses and investigators die or become unavailable. Organizing case files is often one of the first steps taken in cold case investigations. How information was originally recorded becomes very important. No single observation is precise; many variable factors, known and unknown, can alter by minutes, hours, days, weeks, months, or *years* the estimated times of critical events.[74]

Research from 2020 makes an important observation and purports a superior concept: Police cold case teams should consider the incorporation of forensic scientists from not only government agencies, but also academia, within the review team in order to confront the challenges associated with unsolved cases. To best equip cold case investigations for success, a team of experts from both investigative and scientific backgrounds should be tasked to a case. We would not expect one single person to build a complicated structure like a jet plane and we should not expect the same of complex, unsolved cases. Instead, it takes teams of many experts to assemble a plane as no-one would ever suggest a single person should know every intricate detail of every minute component. In the same way, specialist teams working complex cold cases should use a multi-talent approach to resolve these crimes and secure justice for victims and their families.[75]

74 R. Ford, "Critical Times in Murder Investigation (Time of Assault, Incapacitation, and Death)," *The Journal of Criminal Law, Criminology, and Police Science* 43, no. 5 (1953): 672–678.
75 B. Chapman, D. Keatley, G. Oatley, J. Coumbaros, and G. Maker, "A Review and Recommendations for the Integration of Forensic Expertise within Police Cold Case Reviews," *Journal of Criminal Psychology* 10, no. 2 (2020): 79–91.

Charts, Chronologies, and Graphs

Demonstrative material is always helpful in homicide investigations as a means to update, remind, include, and keep all investigators in the loop as the case progresses.

I used to take butcher paper and tape it on the wall with the pertinent information, precautionary instructions, or data I wanted our team to know. We had to ensure we had a secure area to operate, and our messages were out of the view of people not involved in the case.

Many times, we used a PowerPoint projector to illuminate leads-management system information onto a screen or wall where other investigators could glean information and see the progression of the investigation in real time.

Homicide investigations generate large and diverse data in the form of witness interview transcripts, physical evidence, photographs, DNA, and so forth. Homicide case chronologies are summaries of these data created by investigators that consist of short text-based entries documenting specific steps taken in the investigation. A chronology tracks the evolution of an investigation, including when and how persons involved and items of evidence became part of a case; performing named-entity recognition to determine witnesses, suspects, and detectives from chronology entries; using keyword expansion to identify documentary, physical, and forensic evidence in each entry; and linking entities and evidence to construct a homicide investigation knowledge graph.[76]

Utility of Technologies as Investigative Tools

Technological tools are both important and beneficial to the investigator. Technology will never replace the engagement, interview, and collection of facts from people. *We must remember that the utility of technologies and traditional investigative acts should support each other in a waltz together through the context of the facts in the case.* Simultaneous efforts trump single investigative

76 R. Pandey, P. J. Brantingham, C. D. Uchida, and G. Mohler, "Building Knowledge Graphs of Homicide Investigation Chronologies," in *2020 International Conference on Data Mining Workshops*, ed. First Name Last Name (City of Publication: Sorrento, Italy IEEE, 2020): 790–798.

focus by managing the precious time in the case more effectively. Moreover, use of technology should comply with agency policy, investigative reasonableness, individual privacy rights, and the law.

Some examples of these important technologies:

- Polygraph

- Advanced DNA technologies

- CODIS database utility

- Genome sequencing (commercial DNA databases)

- Recent advancements in forensic tools regarding microbiome technologies (specific species of micro communities of bacteria, fungi, and virus) for characteristics of soil, decomposition, or human deposits.

- EnCase examination of hard drives, solid state drives, and other portable digital storage devices or media

- Cloud inventory and analysis

- Geofencing software systems (location information that is being constantly collected and stored by various companies, primarily for research and marketing purposes)

- Cell phone examination (data, locations, tracking, history, and records)

- Databases and data-management systems (highways, tag readers, etc.)

- Digital photography resources (Ring doorbells, CCTV, other security camera systems, etc.)

- Drones

- Laser-driven 3D model creation units (total station surveying, photogrammetry, and other laser-scanning technologies)

- Other geographic information systems that analyze and display specific geographically referenced information that uses data that is attached to a unique location

- Explainable machine learning framework[77] (machine learning models are generated by analyzing vast amounts of historical data, identifying correlations and trends between key data points, and using those insights to make accurate predictions about people's behavior)

- Facial recognition technologies

The Importance of Checklists in Homicide Case Investigations

Levels of cognitive function are often compromised with increasing levels of stress and fatigue, as is often the norm in certain complex, high-intensity fields of work. Aviation, aeronautics, and product manufacturing have come to rely heavily on checklists to aid in reducing human error. The checklist is an important tool in error management across all these fields, contributing significantly to reductions in the risk of costly mistakes and improving overall outcomes.[78]

The same is true for our efforts to work through the many distractions under time restraints in homicide investigations. I carried one of Vernon Geberth's *Practical Homicide Investigation* checklists and field guide for years as a checklist highlighting the key points necessary for a thorough and

---

77   G. M. Campedelli, "Explainable Machine Learning for Predicting Homicide Clearance in the United States," *Journal of Criminal Justice* 79 (2022): 101898.

78   B. M. Hales and P. J. Pronovost, "The Checklist—a Tool for Error Management and Performance Improvement," *Journal of Critical Care* 21, no. 3 (2006): 231–235.

complete investigation. The first section of this book captured Dr. Carter's findings regarding the value of checklist in those agencies that performed well.

I have found that there are two types of checklists. The first example is a standard checklist printed early on that captures broad procedures in very specific and narrowly tailored steps to ensure we do not miss things during our work in homicide investigation (like Geberth's checklist).[79] The second checklist is a narrative document that is created *during* a particular active investigation that focuses on documenting important issues or pending priorities to ensure they will not be overlooked or forgotten during the investigative process.

I created my own checklist in a reporter's notebook at every case I worked or supervised to ensure I did not forget or miss any base I needed to cover.

Then there is an operational best-practice-type list. Not a checklist but a practice plan to assist in the orderly progression from the early to late stages of an investigation. The below sixteen points are an example.

In summary

There are sixteen points regarding the lead investigator/detective's management of an investigation.[80] Central is the lead investigator's ability to manage the case in such fashion that it progresses from general to specific in leaving no stone unturned. Investigative progression should be as swift as practicable while tempered by the operational guardrails and investigative realities of the case. Homicide investigations must be thorough, accurate, and complete. Proper planning, organization, coordination, discipline, and oversight are essential.

These sixteen points are as follows:

---

79 Geberth, *Practical Homicide Investigation Checklist and Field Guide (Practical Aspects of Criminal and Forensic Investigations)*, 2nd ed. (Boca Raton, Florida: CRC Press, 2013).

80 M. J. Sullivan, "Managing Major Case Investigations: Suggestions for Supervisors," *FBI Law Enforcement Bulletin* 67, no. 1 (1998): 1. Addition from: Edwards, J.B. (2005). Georgia law enforcement command college. Columbus State University. Major Case Management.

1. Slow down the pace of the investigation.

   a. Set the example: when the lead investigator is calm, others become calm.

   b. Ensure everyone is thoughtful and think objectively in a very contextually appropriate manner (look before you leap and reserve judgment until facts are available).

   c. Preach being deliberate to the specifics in everything.

   d. Remain aware and prepared to adapt to circumstances that will demand and influence investigators to move fast on particular leads while pausing on others.

   e. The chief investigator is responsible to let the facts drive the pace of the investigation, not subjective influences.

2. Use all resources available

   a. Utilize all available personnel early; the early phases of a homicide investigation are critically important and personnel intensive.

   b. Do not hesitate to call in more resources.

   c. Harness the ability, experience, and expertise of other divisions within or outside agencies (state and federal).

   d. Establish a multijurisdictional task force model if needed.

   e. Ensure the ability and expertise of investigators match the assignments given.

3. Plan, organize, and develop your checklist.

a. Develop a standing list of tasks that must be performed.

b. The checklist needs to be ongoing, up to date, and comprehensive.

c. Prioritize issues and action steps to be addressed.

d. Make notes of pending obligations and responsibilities.

e. Maintain evidence issues lists.

f. Document significant communications with stakeholders.

g. Document significant reports and case-pertinent information from briefings.

4. Focus on the evidence.

a. Ensure the evidence is located and obtained legally. Communicate, coordinate, and cooperate with prosecutors at the beginning.

b. Remember there is no crime scene exception to the Fourth Amendment.

c. Don't let events sidetrack or prevent attention to probable evidence recovery issues or identified evidence located.

d. Evaluate articulable suspicion and probable cause issues before detention or arrest.

e. Make investigators think about "conviction evidence" versus "arrest evidence." Don't let a short-term fix cause a long-term embarrassment.

    f. Ensure scenes are thoroughly examined, inventoried, and held until after the autopsy or as long as needed.

    g. Ensure things are done right the first time because *you don't get another chance.*

5. Know your scenes.

    a. Familiarize yourself with the crime scene(s).

    b. Ensure scenes have the security required.

    c. Use video as the gateway to enter scenes virtually to prevent contamination from others. Remember Locard's Exchange Principle: "*Everyone* takes something in and something out at a crime scene."

        i. Contamination issues cause big problems.

        ii. Major cases attract high-ranking visitors.

    d. Manage your scene, control your scene, and protect your scene (utilize digital photos or video to let others see things).

6. Keep a notebook.

    a. Document your observations and questions.

    b. Keep notes documenting all actions, directives, observations, communications, and events.

    c. Ensure times and dates are accurate.

    d. *This will serve as a timeline of events for later testimony in court.*

    e.   Ensure access to the lead assignments (use a leads-management system).

7. Insulate your staff from outside issues

    a.   Ensure fact inventory and investigator knowledge continuity as the case progresses in time.

    b.   Ensure chain of command is briefed going up and coming down within your appropriate ability.

    c.   Shield investigators from the media and others that sidetrack them.

    d.   Help coordinate proactively with pending court appearances from other cases.

8. Conduct at least two briefings per day.

    a.   Have a secure location for an early briefing and late briefing for all investigators.

    b.   Include crime scene investigators and MEs.

    c.   Details, facts, and information will be *shared* and *compared* with all investigators.

    d.   Apply contextual feature drilling and nuance-sensitive debate.

    e.   Make sure lead management is in place and functional to every investigator.

    f.   Preach to stay focused.

g. Issues will be evaluated and tested objectively by investigators playing the devil's advocate.

h. Set your priorities (order of doing and time sensitive).

i. Set your objectives (what to do and when in the context of the whole case).

j. Assignments made through documented lead distribution.

k. Ensure congruency with your investigator's assignments (reinterviews, associated leads, etc.).

l. Follow-up leads analyzed and call-in coordination with the chief investigator

m. Times are set to overlap shifts for information and investigative strategy and tactic congruency (if running twenty-four seven).

9. Keep supervisors and command staff plugged in.

a. Ensure supervisory sitreps and regular briefings.

b. Invite command representatives to attend investigative briefings.

c. Keep your boss plugged in.

d. Communicate problematic issues ahead of time when first forecasted.

e. Do not provide a problem without your recommendation for a solution.

f. Remember that bad news does not get better with age.

10. Communicate with prosecutors.

   a. Never surprise your prosecutor; notify them when a homicide occurs in their jurisdiction.

   b. Involving prosecutors in the beginning of the case benefits both the investigation and later court prosecution.

   c. Prosecutors can provide advice and assistance that often can provide a more legally sound and efficient investigative effort.

   d. Prosecutors are valuable in their assistance in search warrants and other court orders.

   e. Remember ownership theory in the case. If prosecutors are a part of the case, they feel some ownership in its progression.

11. Cooperate with media.

   a. Be professional and sensitive toward the media's role and responsibilities.

   b. Be polite and kind.

   c. Work through a PIO if possible. (Command should have the PIO manage the media.)

   d. All case-specific information needs to be vetted through the lead investigator before any release by *anyone*.

   e. Monitor or have the PIO watch social media to stay ahead of media issues.

f. Manage the media while protecting and controlling sensitive information by providing them a generic (nonspecific) sound bite or video opportunity.

g. Be truthful, and never deceive the media. Advise them it is inappropriate to release specific details in an active ongoing case.

h. Always return their phone calls (key phrase: "It would be inappropriate for me to comment regarding specific investigative context in an active ongoing case").

i. Use the media if required. But have the infrastructure and plan needed to handle incoming information.

12. Monitor and provide for the welfare of all investigators, CSI, and other staff.

a. Ensure sound perimeters with officers at guard for safety and security.

b. Ensure access to clean restrooms.

c. Have food and drink on station.

d. Provide the opportunity for breaks.

e. Ensure reasonable comfort within the climate or working environment.

f. Ensure communications are available.

g. *Praise people for their efforts.*

13. Manage the ongoing investigation.

   a. Maintain and sustain investigative discipline within the operational context.

      i. Ask "How do we know that?" to test assumptions and hear the underlying circumstances articulated to other investigators.

      ii. Ensure assignments match strategy and fit the individual investigator.

      iii. Ensure overall congruency in all case matters.

   b. Cast vision regarding the requirement for specificity, and stress the importance of seizing the initiative.

   c. Keep the case momentum moving forward.

   d. Weigh all probable consequences, and test fact patterns.

   e. Don't micromanage.

   f. Give specific praise for specific accomplishments and how they improve the investigation process.

14. Control documents and files.

   a. Ensure the integrity of the case file and the leads-management system.

   b. Require timely documentation, and provide ongoing oversight.

   c. Ensure the leads-management system is documented, accurate, up to date, and complete.

    d. Ensure proper evidence and property documentation and storage.

    e. Check leads for a match to the appropriate documentation in reports.

15. Manage and cooperate with stakeholders.

    a. Provide support and care to the victim's families and friends.

    b. Communicate (keep them in the loop).

    c. Share information when appropriate.

    d. Remain sensitive to community anxiety or fear regarding open homicide cases.

    e. Use victim/witness coordinators.

    f. Use churches, Red Cross, and other nonprofits if needed to provide tangible human assistance.

16. Insulate the integrity of sensitive case information.

    a. Ensure secure or encrypted communications if needed.

    b. Use covert assembly of investigators if needed.

    c. Ensure document, computer, and data security.

    d. Limit access and knowledge when necessary.

    e. Use precautionary instruction and consequence notification regarding information integrity.

f. Secure environments.

g. Logs, documentation, and memoranda to ensure accountability.

h. Apply Prophylactic guidance and advice to victims and witnesses about talking with those outside the investigation.

i. Make a judicial request for temporary sealing of affidavits for search warrants and other sensitive court orders for articulable case integrity reasons.

j. Have a sound leak policy in place that everyone has been put on notice regarding its content.

Investigative Failures (Lessons Learned) from Past Cases

The best crystal ball is often a rearview mirror.
—Unknown

It's necessary to be slightly underemployed if you are doing something significant.
—Dr. James Watson

The way we investigate and how we investigate become major components in the success or failure of criminal cases.
—Author

Critical to an investigation is the amount of information collected and its accuracy. "Quantity must have quality" information must be both thorough & credible. More often than not, preliminary information is froth with inaccuracy. Important judgments and decisions will be based upon the *interpretation* of the information at hand. Facts and fact patterns must be *interpreted accurately*. Decisions must be made based upon the facts of each case. The investigation must go where *sound and objective* facts lead it.

The question becomes…is what causes competent and dedicated investigators to make avoidable mistakes jeopardizing the successful resolution of their case? If we don't understand investigative failures and their causes, then we are doomed to repeat them.
—Dr. Kim Rossmo[81]

Poor methods utilized by investigators, or investigative teams, often lead to investigative failures that cannot be cured and missed opportunities that the investigation can never recover from.

A constant and ongoing theme in this book has focused on the fact that investigative narratives of homicides are co-constructed by a variety of actors, including detectives, scientists, and prosecutors.

They are told and retold within the investigation phase, as they are assembled, arranged, rearranged, and shaped into one coherent and plausible narrative. All of the actors' impressions, experiences, and expectations of what kind of homicide has been committed frame how they construct these emerging narratives. The emerging investigation's homicide case narratives are polyphonic and merge many voices. Whose voices are heard and how they are represented are critical elements of the narrative homicide investigation construction process. The notion to abandon theory or reformulate theories is an emerging and ongoing progressive process in the case narrative that becomes the focus and defines the scope of the investigation.[82]

---

81 Kim Rossmo (lecture, Forsyth, GA, Georgia Public Safety Training Center to the Georgia Bureau of Investigation, 2007).

82 F. Brookman, H. Jones, R. Williams, and J. Fraser, "Crafting Credible Homicide Narratives: Forensic Technoscience in Contemporary Criminal Investigations," *Deviant Behavior* 43, no. 3 (2022): 340–366.

In the end, within the adversarial trial that characterizes many criminal justice systems, it is not the truth that is contested; rather it is the veracity, plausibility, and persuasiveness of the competing narratives of prosecution and defense, all mindful that prosecutors look for truth while jurors look for doubt.

Much of homicide investigation requires the chief investigator to take on the role as the information manager. During the fast-paced progression of the investigation, officers work tirelessly to identify, collect, and interpret fact patterns and evidence. Then they work quickly to make inferences and deductions from the complicated, complex, and contextually rich information. They work in a time-sensitive environment under circumstances that create tremendous pressure to solve the case. Under the best of conditions, their interpretation of investigative findings is often ambiguous, uncertain, and subjective.

All of these factors influence the investigators' role in making important judgments and trying to make informed decisions. The combination of ambiguous, uncertain information in unpredictable, time-sensitive environments significantly influences an investigator's judgments and impacts decisions that may increase the risk of errors in these types of cases.

Many investigative failures have been attributed to coercive interrogations, poor eyewitness identification technique, unreliable witness accounts and narratives of the suspect(s), and poor interviewing skills. When investigations go wrong, however, it is an even more fundamental feature of the investigations that seems to fail—namely, the detectives' judgments, decision-making, and overall supervision of the case. A common denominator can be noted between different accounts of criminal investigative failures: investigators strive to confirm their initial hypothesis, while seemingly ignoring or downplaying conflicting information. The investigative psychology is primarily directed toward the detectives' cognitive tasks, such as the processing of information, the identification of different investigative scenarios, and decisions on the best investigative strategies or lines of inquiry.[83]

---

83 I. A. Fahsing, *The Making of an Expert Detective: Thinking and Deciding in Criminal Investigations* (Ineko, Sweden: University of Gothenburg, 2016).

Dr. Kim Rossmo focuses on three reasons of ineffective investigative thinking: cognitive biases, organizational traps, and lack of understanding of probabilities. The research of criminal investigative failures provides some insight into what can go wrong.

Dr. Kim Rossmo and Dr. Joycelyn Pollock[84] classified causes using a scheme for error analysis adapted from Reason's (1990) failure domains:

- Personal issues

- Organizational problems

- Situational features

    Personal issues were individual-level problems, such as poor decision-making or flawed judgment (e.g., confirmation bias, misfeasance). Organizational problems were located in the structure, procedures, training, or resources of the police agency (e.g., groupthink, poor supervision). Situational factors were environmental features or characteristics of the crime, external to the control of the police or government (e.g., stranger crime, media frenzy).

    Personal factors, in particular, a rush to judgment, tunnel vision, and confirmation bias, were found to be the most common causes (61%) of criminal investigative failures. A crime can only be solved through evidence: a witness, a confession, or physical evidence.

    An unsolved crime, or an incorrectly solved crime (wrongful conviction), is therefore fundamentally a failure of evidence—its collection, evaluation, or analysis.

---

84   D. K. Rossmo, and J. M. Pollock, "Confirmation Bias and Other Systemic Causes of Wrongful Convictions: A Sentinel Events Perspective," *NEULR* 11 (2019): 790.

Evidence collection involves locating eyewitnesses, interviewing people, recovering physical evidence from the crime scene, and similar efforts. Evaluating evidence is the determination of its accuracy or truthfulness. Analysis includes extracting information from the evidence, determining relationships, and developing patterns.

Evidence evaluation and analysis issues are the more common causes of investigative failure. Breakdowns in evidence collection were much less important unless they co-occurred with evaluation or analysis problems.

Although detectives typically have a good appreciation of the technical nature of evidence, they do not always fully understand its probabilistic structure.

Evidence has both significance and reliability. Significance is defined as the ratio of the probability of the evidence given the suspect's guilt to the probability of the evidence given the suspect's innocence. It is therefore necessary to determine not only how strongly the evidence supports the guilt of a suspect or points toward a particular theory of the crime but also the viability of other explanations for the evidence.

Reliability is the accuracy or truthfulness of the evidence. Evidence must be evaluated to determine the likelihood that it is true or accurate. All evidence has an error rate: An eyewitness might misidentify a suspect, a person may make a false confession, or a scientific test can produce a false positive. Unfortunately, we tend to place more importance on significant evidence even if its reliability is low. Low reliability, however, undermines significance strength; detectives first need to estimate the reliability of an item of evidence before determining how much weight it should be given. As the possibility of mistakes and human error always exists, source reliability, forensic test error rates, evidentiary consistency/trustworthiness data, and any other known issues should be considered.

Evidence is not more reliable simply because the investigator wants it to be and is not less reliable because it is inconsistent with the prevailing investigative theory.

Rossmo and Pollock recommend investigators and detectives need to consider questions of significance, reliability, independence, and patterns (SRIP):

- What is the significance of the evidence?

- How strongly does it point toward the guilt of a suspect or a particular theory of the crime in comparison with other suspects or theories?

- What is the reliability of this evidence?

- How accurate or truthful is it? (Even if the evidence is significant, it will have little probative value if it is wrong.)

- How independent is the evidence?

- Does it provide a unique contribution, or is it merely derivative of already existing evidence? (Evidence that lacks independence may not contribute any additional information to an investigation.)

- How does the evidence fit in with what else is known in the investigation—its overall information pattern? (Evidence in an investigation should not be cherry-picked but must be considered in a holistic fashion.)

Different items of evidence may point the investigation in various directions, and these inconsistencies must be considered and reasoned through by the investigators asking thoughtful questions supported by critical thinking.

Rossmo and Pollock caution that danger arises when one of the four SRIP questions is ignored because an investigator suffers from cognitive bias. By asking these questions, and considering their answers, detectives may avoid the more egregious evidence errors and reduce the risk of a criminal investigative failure.

Here are four areas that complement the above research where critical mistakes are made that are detrimental to the homicide investigation.

1. Fact-Finding

Many problems and failures in homicide investigations often begin and result from poor fact-finding methods:

- Nonspecific, incomplete, less than thorough interviews with witnesses, victims or suspects

- Judgments made during the investigation without the investigator evaluating all the facts available

- Poor communications between investigators, the lead investigator, supervisors, and managers

- Poor investigative strategy and tactics based on assumptions that are not verified

- Failure to interview the necessary people or not interviewing everyone who may know something

- Too much stock in one interview (especially beware of the in-custody witness or inmate/convict)

- Incomplete or poorly documented statements by witnesses, victims, or suspects that

  - are nonspecific to events, incidents, people, and factual contexts;

  - have no corroboration; or

  - involve credibility problems with witnesses (impeachable).

- Failure to properly review, examine, evaluate, and interpret all the evidence and fact patterns in the totality of the entire case.

- Poor documentation or no oversight review for exculpatory or Brady material.

- No specific knowledge for questions or communications with polygraph examiners.

2. Poor Investigative Strategy and Tactical Development

- Jurisdiction/authority issues

- The investigation exceeds the scope of prosecution (and the law)

- Poor investigative tactics (marginal or illegal)

- Lack of direction or vision by chief investigator or management

- Poor communication among investigators, MEs, CSI, lab, and prosecutors involved

- Resources do not support required operations (not enough investigators or support staff)

- Witness credibility or location issues (impeachable or nomadic)

- Failure to recognize problematic issues with Brady, Bruton, Giglio, or Crawford v. Washington rules

- Premature arrest

- Poor eyewitness identification procedures

3. Poor Organization, Structures, or Procedures

- Failure to plan, prepare, and train

- Failure to identify "up front" roles and responsibilities

- Failure to identify, process, and run leads quickly

- Failure to analyze and follow up on leads

- Failure to manage those roles and responsibilities to ensure "investigative discipline"

- Failure to communicate properly

- Failure to manage large volumes of information effectively and efficiently

- Failure to document timely and properly

4. Poor or Lack of Forensic Effort

- Not searching, not finding, not securing, not collecting, not documenting, and not examining

- Poor general-to-specific and broad-scene and area-of-the-scene photography

- No initial scene inventory or final all-encompassing inventory

- Failure to preserve scenes

- Failure to hold scenes until after autopsy or fully completed investigative position

- Failure to address perishable items or issues

- Failure to analyze, compare, and examine evidence in combination with investigative results (from autopsy to lab work to the digital examination of data)

The Five Fatal Process Errors:

- Prejudgment absent all the facts; lack of objectivity where the investigation outruns the evidence

- Lack of specificity in interviews, sketches, notes, and reports

- Lack of thoroughness and completeness in overall investigative process (shortcutting)

- Constitutional violations in investigative process

- Failure to receive commitment to initiate and sustain prosecution

Strategies to Help Avoid Investigative Failures

In his important book *Criminal Investigative Failures*, Dr. Kim Rossmo outlines the many traps and pitfalls that cause failure in investigations. He offers strategies to prevent, mitigate, or reduce mistakes that occur time and time again in these cases.

Six Strategies to Help Avoid Investigative Failures[85]

- Ensure managerial awareness of these problems through case study–based training.

- Encourage an atmosphere of open inquiry, ensuring investigative managers remain impartial and neutral.

- If possible, defer reaching conclusions until sufficient data has been collected.

- Consider different perspectives and encourage cross fertilization of ideas, thereby avoiding tunnel vision.

- Organize brainstorming sessions, and seek creativity rather than consensus.

- Ensure that investigative managers willingly accept objections, doubts, and criticisms from team members.

A final perspective from Dr. Kim Rossmo is very important regarding investigative failures or mistakes. Rossmo states,

---

85 D. K. Rossmo, "Criminal Investigative Failures," *FBI Law Enforcement Bulletin* 75, no. 10 (2006): 12.

"Police investigators are routinely expected to solve a case quickly and move on to the next crime—often within 48 hours. But production pressures can undermine detective work. Undiscovered evidence cannot be analyzed, plays no role in the search for suspects, and will never be used to convict an offender. Time constraints jeopardize accurate reliability assessments and encourage cognitive biases. Resource limitations translate into evidence that is not fully analyzed in the forensics laboratory or in the minds of detectives." [86]

It is far easier to fix things at the front end rather than the rear end. Investigators must sustain the operational awareness to recognize and identify potential problem issues early to resolve them under manageable conditions before they can result in bad outcomes.

Problems and bad news do not get better with age. We cannot not prevent every mistake. However, we can limit the frequency with which they occur and the damage they make in our cases. In many investigations the combined effort to make more thoughtful and informed decisions will proactively prevent mistakes and problems by addressing the underlying causes before they can have a chance to adversely impact our case.

---

86   D. K. Rossmo, "Dissecting a Criminal Investigation," *Journal of Police and Criminal Psychology* 36, no. 4 (2021): 639–651.

FINAL THOUGHTS

First and foremost, I wrote this book with the hope and prayer that it would serve as a practical and meaningful resource for the thousands of homicide investigators who serve in the many local, state, and federal law enforcement agencies across this great nation. My goal is to promote the professional growth and development of those charged with the awesome responsibility of securing justice for the victim and bringing justice to the offender in murder cases.

Second, I have been blessed with a wonderful career that provided in-depth experience from working the most complex homicide cases to the simplest while surrounded by the best of the best investigators. When I transferred from Atlanta to Statesboro, I walked into the premier training academy for homicide investigations. A treasured mentor, DA Dupont K. Cheney, provided me two great sayings. "Edwards…it ain't what you want, it's what you've got." And "Edwards…you're in the church, but not in the right pew." Both of these quotes taught me the value of persistence to make a good case. Another of my many mentors, Charles Sikes would say, "film is cheap." In other words, you can't take enough pictures of a scene. This taught me the importance of specific documentation.

Finally, as the special agent in charge of the Statesboro field office, I was blessed to have extraordinary teams of GBI agents that far exceeded in their job and made me so proud to be a small part of their exemplary work as investigators. I remain so appreciative for that experience and the purposeful meaning they gave me. This book was written on that foundation of appreciation to God, my family, the GBI, and all of the lionhearts across the country in federal, state, and local law enforcement agencies responsible for working these important investigations.

"Blessed are the peacemakers, for they will be called children of God."
—Matthew 5:9

God bless and keep you in your endeavors to carry out the good Lord's work!
—John B. Edwards Sr., 2022